To those whose lives have been impacted by incarceration and are struggling for hope, this book is dedicated to you.

This book is also dedicated to the men and women who have experienced incarceration, have fought hard to overcome, and have shared their thoughts and stories of reentry and renewal within the pages of this devotional. You have faced challenges that most people cannot even imagine. Your journey has included fighting through obstacles and setbacks. Yours has been a road of rebuilding your life and discovering a new future through the hope and grace of God's love.

This book is a testament to the strength and resilience you found in Christ. It is a witness to the moments you felt most hopeless and alone, and discovered you were not. This book is your testimony to the truths you have learned through God's love and the care you received through the people He brought into your life to help you.

Thank you for sharing your stories with me. I am honored to have the opportunity to tell them.

I hope this book will inspire the hopeful and the hopeless. I hope it will provide the encouragement and resources God has provided to succeed. I hope it will help you to find the new future God has planned for you.

Forward

Scott Kelley spent over ten years of his life in prison. He spent many more in and out of jail, lost in a life of addiction. But, no more! Today Scott serves as a mentor and a musician with Freedom Life. His passion is to share with everyone his secret to life recovery and transformation. His secret is actually a person. That person is Jesus Christ.

While in prison, Scott would cry out to Jesus for help and Jesus would be there to meet him. Through these moments of humbled connection with Jesus, Scott has written many songs. Scott now sings some of these songs as lead singer of "Heart Cry," a music ministry team of Freedom Life. God moves powerfully through his songs and his testimony.

One very powerful song that God has used to touch many lives is entitled, "40 Days." The Chorus of this song is:

"40 days, 40 nights,
and it's plain to see that this world ain't right.
Well He hung a rainbow in the sky,
and He's watching over you and I.
40 days, 40, nights,
and He's still, today, reigning in my life.
I was a sinner who was lost and found.
Well I once was blind but I can see now.
40 days!"

My prayer is that God will use this "40 Day" devotional in your life as powerfully as we have seen God use Scott's song, "40 Days" in many lives.

In the Bible, "40 days and 40 nights," is very noteworthy. The number 40 appears 146 times in scripture. The term "40 days" or "40 days and 40 nights" appears twenty-four times. Each time it is used, it is referring to a highly significant timeframe of seeking, testing, trial, instruction, or judgment. It also can represent a period of engagement and completion when it comes to meaningful workings between God and individuals, His people, or the world as a whole.

This does not mean that God only works in periods of time that measure 40. Scripture is filled with workings of God that were far less or longer than 40 days, nights, or years. However, it does mean that the number 40 has significance when emphasizing a great work or movement of God. It means pay attention, something deeply profound is happening.

What "40 days and 40 nights" means to me personally is that God is alive and active. He knows, He cares, and He is engaged in the smallest and greatest details and needs of my life. The same God who created this world and has been deeply involved in all that has taken place in scripture and in world history, is also present and deeply involved in me. It is an invitation from God to me, to us, to join with Him in a journey that "will" change our lives.

Through Jesus, God invites us to receive Him and to allow Him to lead us through seasons of opportunity, growth, and spiritual transformation. Yes, some of these seasons are difficult and trying. We can find ourselves in the midst of struggles that feel overwhelming and even hopeless. However, "40 days and 40 nights" says to me, "Hold on!" As Psalms 30:5 says, *"weeping may endure for a night, but joy comes in the morning."*

Jesus went through many seasons of suffering and growth in His life. Yes, He was and is God, but He was also flesh and human as we are. He came into sufferings of flesh so He could enter into our fleshly sufferings with amazing grace, love, healing, and transformation. He was even arrested and suffered prison so He could enter into our imprisonment. Hebrews 5:8-9 tells us that, *"though He was a Son, yet He learned obedience by the things which He suffered. And having been perfected, He became the source of eternal salvation for all those who obey Him."*

Jesus spent 40 days and 40 nights suffering as he fasted in the desert. He endured powerful attacks from Satan while in a very weakened state. Through this season of testing and trial, Jesus defeated Satan in the desert. Christs' victory over Satan in the desert gave Him seasoned power to defeat Satan through the mockery of an unjust trial, the torture He faced in wrongful incarceration, and the sufferings He faced on the cross. After His resurrection, Jesus spent 40 days fellowshipping with and instructing His disciples. As Christ won eternal victory through the cross, He now invites us into that same victory through the cross He leads us to face in our lives.

I do not know where you are personally in your life. I do not know what areas of struggle or suffering you may be facing. Maybe you are sitting in a jail cell feeling overwhelmed and hopeless. Perhaps you are in a prison facility having to walk every day in the midst of an environment of great stress, intimidation, humiliation, and powerlessness. You might be a family member of someone who is incarcerated and you are struggling with conflicting emotions of need, anger, longing, and uncertainty. Perhaps you are someone who has never faced incarceration, but you are still human, and to be human is to face a battlefield of sin and struggle.

Regardless, I pray that as you take a journey through this 40 Days Devotional, you will experience the intimate presence of God with you. I pray that the thoughts and stories of so many here at Freedom Life who have shared from their own struggles in the devotions they have written, will be used by God to touch your life and encourage your faith. Every daily devotion was written by someone who themselves faced suffering seasons of incarceration and hopelessness. You can read their stories of overcoming experience with God in the back of this devotional.

Above all, I pray you will come to experience that God loves you more than you could possibly know. God is reaching out to you in whatever season of struggle you are facing to say, *"Come to me all who are weary and burdened, and I will give you rest."* Whatever you are facing. Whatever you are feeling. You are not alone! You do not have to be alone! Whether you are in an actual prison cell, or trapped inside a prison or within yourself, I pray you will hear His voice and receive Him into your heart. I pray He will turn your season of suffering into an eternal season of new life. May the next "40 days" of your life be filled with "faith, hope, and love".

May you be able to say and sing, "Well I once was blind but I can see now." "40 Days!"

Danny Hampton, Executive Director

You can hear the song "40 Days" by streaming the Heart Cry Album on all platforms.

Heart Cry

The journey of Heart Cry began in 2010. Danny Hampton, after serving over 20 years in church pastoral ministry, was called to serve as a prison chaplain at the Marion Correctional Institution in McDowell County. While serving, God began to move powerfully in the lives of the men serving on the prison ministry worship team in the Marion Correctional Minimum Security Unit. The worship team began to spend time not only in music practice, but in prayer and Bible study.

In November 2012, a nonprofit ministry, called "Freedom Life" was incorporated to minister to the needs of current or formerly incarcerated men and women. The worship team was also granted permission to go outside the prison on ministry concert trips and became known as, "Heart Cry."

The group is now composed of Danny Hampton, Scott Kelley, Melissa Lister, Michael Fox and Stephen Hampton. "With Me All Along," the title track of the album, is an original song written by member Scott Kelley while in prison. It was the first song Heart Cry learned and performed in concerts when the group was first forming inside the walls of the correctional institution. All of Kelley's original songs included on this project were written while he was in prison.

Through the power of song, Heart Cry has seen God bring hope to many lives that, because of a deeply broken past and destructive choices, have struggled to believe that they could truly be worth loving. Their songs represent the stories of God's healing love and transformation in their own lives.

Danny Hampton stated, "We hope that God will bring healing and new hope to the lives of so many that are desperate to believe that their lives can be made new, regardless of where or what they have been through. Seeing God's love bring hope to so many lives trapped in hopelessness is what has inspired this project. We pray that through this project many more lives will find new hope and life through God's love."

Jim Smith, Development Director of Freedom Life Ministries and an avid Heart Cry supporter said of their recent performance, "I was engaged by their use of different styles of music. It helps to reach a wide range of listeners and the testimonies given really made the songs come to life. It helped me realize how powerful addiction can be, but also how recovery and healing is possible."

You can search for "With Me All Along" on all streaming platforms. This album can be purchased on iTunes or Amazon Music.

Several reentry testimonies can be found on page 104

Index

56	Romans 5:1-5	Janis Bolick
59	Isaiah 30:21	Melissa Marlowe
61	Psalms 68:19	Paul Cole
63	Psalms 27:5	Anita Miller
65	Jeremiah 33:8	Anthony Collins
67	Isaiah 38:20	Ashley McPeters
69	James 2:18-20	Chris Cordero
72	Isaiah 51:11	Doug Hall
74	Philippians 4:6	Kim Wilkerson
77	2 Corinthians 12:9	Janis Bolick
81	Psalms 121:2-3	Jason Wallace
83	Psalms 18:27-28	Robin Stapleton
85	Proverbs 2:6	Jeff Wardsworth
87	1 Peter 2:9	Julie McAllister
89	Psalms 30:5	Karen MacKinnon
93	John 3:16	Kim Brown
95	Romans 8:11	Paul Cole
97	John 14:2-3	Janis Bolick
100	Psalms 149:4	Kim Miller
102	John 10:28	Jim Smith

God's Plan is Good

For I know the plans I have for you, declares the LORD,
plans for welfare and not for evil,
to give you a future and a hope.
Jeremiah 29:11

This verse is one of the most beloved and well-known verses in the Bible. It is a promise from God that He has good plans for us, even when things are tough.

The context of this verse is that Jeremiah is prophesying to the Israelites who have been exiled to Babylon. They are in a difficult situation, and they are wondering if God has abandoned them. But Jeremiah assures them that God is still with them, and that He has good plans for their future.

This verse is a reminder that God is always with us, even when we are going through difficult times. He has good plans for us, and He will never leave us or forsake us.

Some things to think about:
- Remember that God is with you. He is always there, even when you can't feel Him.
- Trust in God's promises. He has said that He has good plans for you, so believe Him.
- Don't give up hope. God is working in your life, even when you can't see it.
- Keep praying. Talk to God about your struggles, and ask Him for His help.
- Find a community of believers. Surround yourself with people who will support you and pray for you.

How you can apply this to your life: Are you facing any difficult times? If so, remember that God is with you, and He has good plans for you. Trust in His promises, don't give up hope, and keep praying. You can also find a community of believers who can support you and pray for you.

Digging deeper: Jeremiah 29:13-14: *"You will seek me and find me when you seek me with all your heart, I will be found by you," declares the LORD, "and I will restore your fortunes and gather you from all the nations and all the places where I have driven you", declares the LORD, "and I will bring you back to the place from which I sent you into exile."*

How you can pray about this: Dear God, Thank YOU for Your promise that you have good plans for me. I know that I can trust You, even when things are tough. Help me to keep my hope alive, and to keep praying. I know you are working in my life, and I will trust that You will bring good out of my struggles. Amen

Remember this: Now is the time to seek him!

Jim Smith is the Development Director for Freedom Life and is owner of WJS Creative Group.

Giving Up Control to God

Commit to the Lord whatever you do,
and He will establish your plans.
Proverbs 16:3

Completely giving our decisions, along with our lives to Christ translates into us giving up what we want and letting Him show us what He wants us to do. If we fully commit to God, He promises to not only establish our plans, but put them into our hearts.

For years, my wife and I made plans that once she was able to retire from her job, we were going to move to the mountains of western North Carolina. Our plans included playing some golf, reading, and just enjoying our days to do whatever we wanted.

As it turns out, this was not God's plan for our lives. Instead of lazy days, I found myself volunteering at prisons and at a local outreach ministry and she spends most of her time volunteering at our church.

A lot of folks feel like they are losing control of their lives, but what they are actually doing is being closer to God by allowing Him to direct their paths. God cannot and will not carry out His work through a person whose heart is disobedient or proud.

Jeff Wardsworth

Some things to think about:
- God promises to establish our plans
- We must have obedient hearts in order for God to work through us
- Remember to allow for God's plans and not seek to convince God of our plans

How you can apply this to your life: It is important for us to ask the Spirit to examine our hearts and reveal to us the areas where we are not being obedient. We must also remember that just because we have good plans does not mean they are God's plans.

Digging deeper: Isaiah 55:8-9: *"For my thoughts are not your thoughts, neither are your ways my ways," declares the LORD. "As the heavens are higher than the earth, so are my ways higher than your ways and my thoughts than your thoughts."*

How you can pray about this: Lord Jesus, soften our hearts so that we can learn to be obedient to Your plan. Holy Spirit, help us to see You more clearly so that we allow You to free us from trying to control everything. Thank You for Your plans for us.

Remember this: Giving God control of your life will set you free!

Let God Work

Do not be deceived: God is not mocked,
for whatever one sows, that will he also reap.
Galatians 6:7

Letting the Lord work isn't always easy. Especially in a society that has to have everything right now! I spent seventeen years making a wreck of my life. I have only been on the straight and narrow for five and a half years.

If you go out and plant a garden, you're not going to harvest your crop the next day. You're going to have to sow your crop, be faithful in watering it, and keep the weeds out. That's exactly how it is with our lives.

When we have sown to the flesh for years. We have a lot of bad crops we must deal with. Like heartache, broken relationships, jail/prison time, debt, trust issues, things like losing your license.

All of these are bad crops that I have personally experienced from my past. In fact, I lost everything that I had, but that isn't the end of my story, and it doesn't have to be the end of yours.

If you will believe in the Lord Jesus Christ. Accept and ask Him into your heart the benefits are innumerable! Once you have done this your life can really begin!

You may be dealing with that bad fruit this very moment but trust me when I say if it isn't good, it isn't over (that is if you're sowing good seed). You're not going to start harvesting the good crop until it has time to grow.

It takes time to grow in the Lord. It's going to take getting in the word of God and watering your spirit. God will give the increase.

Steven Davis

Some things to think about:
- It takes time to straighten your life out after years of addiction
- When you accept the Lord Jesus into your life His Spirit will help you sow good seed
- The harvest comes in the Lord's timing

How you can apply this to your life: Take time to grow in your relationship with Jesus. Allow Him to guide you and be patient. As your relationship with Jesus grows stronger, you will feel His Spirit strengthening you and giving you peace.

Digging deeper: Galatians 6:8-9 *For the one who sows to his own flesh will from the flesh reap corruption, but the one who sows to the Spirit will from the Spirit reap eternal life. And let us not grow weary of doing good, for in due season we will reap, if we do not give up.*

How you can pray about this: Lord, show me how to walk more closely with You. Help me to let go of my old habits and addictions and to rejoice in the freedom that You have provided through the cross. Work through me to sow good seeds of hope for salvation

Remember this: Your life changes when you invite Jesus into your heart!

In Control?

For the Spirit God gave us does not make us timid, but gives us power, love and self-discipline.
2 Timothy 1:7 (NIV)

Have you ever felt out of control? Like you just can't stop. If you have driven a car at some point, you most likely felt this like when you lost control of your vehicle on a slick snow-covered road. In this life and in our world, things can often get out of control without the control of the Holy Spirit.

The Apostle Paul is writing this to Timothy, a young man what we would call today as a teenager. You remember those days? We acted in ourselves and that is why we did things that were really out of control. We took risks that as we get older we most likely wouldn't take. Why? Because we wise up or learned the hard way of those risks we took earlier.

Paul was reminding Timothy that as a believer in Jesus, God gave us His Holy Spirit to help us to stay in control of this life. The Spirit doesn't make us timid. This word means coward or fearful. I know what you may be thinking, "I'm not a coward" and "when challenged I'll take the risk". This challenge is not if you would take a risk in the world rather would you take the risk for God?

See we often take risks for our pleasure or to prove something to others, yet when Jesus asks something of us do we then take a risk or do we cower? Like leaving our life for His life, sharing the truth of His word with someone, or praying with someone or going against the world's ways for His way?

The Spirit gives us the power to act. God's strength is the most powerful in all the Universe! Therefore, in Christ you have the power to overcome your addiction or any temptation you face through the power of Jesus. If God can move mountains He can move yours.

How will you walk in the Spirit of the Lord today?

Paul Cole

Some things to think about:
- God gives us His Spirit to help us.
- Are you willing to take a risk for God?
- The power of Christ in you can overcome anything you face.

How you can apply this to your life: It is easy to forget that we are not in control of things. We often forget about the sovereignty of God and try to solve problems on our own. If we can trust God to know what is best we can live our lives with less worry and stress.

Digging deeper: Deuteronomy 31:8 *It is the LORD who goes before you. He will be with you; he will not leave you or forsake you. Do not fear or be dismayed.*

How you can pray about this: Father, thank You for how you go before us in every situation we face. Help us to remember that we can trust You to take care of us and provide all that we need. Forgive us when we seek to be in control instead of surrendering to Your guidance.

Remember this: Nothing can defeat the power of God!

God Meets Our Needs

And my God will supply every need of yours
according to his riches in glory in Christ Jesus.
Philippians 4:19

On May 21, 2022 I went to the hospital for what I thought was a pulled muscle. The ER doctor ran a CT scan and found a mass on my left kidney, spots in my lungs and two cracked ribs.

It happened to be my 58th birthday. The ER doctor wanted to admit me to the hospital that day but I wanted to attend my church celebration because it was the seventh anniversary of our church replant. I wanted to celebrate my birthday with my new church family because I was now the only living sibling out of four in my family.

I attended the church celebration and had to leave because of intense pain. But my church family gathered around me and prayed. I returned to the ER the next morning and they transported me to Asheville, NC Mission campus.

Further testing there revealed two spots on my lungs and bone lesions throughout my body. I felt as though I had been handed a death sentence, but I was ready to meet my Jesus. I was grieving leaving my kids, but also knew God was going to meet all my needs. Biopsies were performed, but my faith stayed in my Jesus.

I knew that no matter what my Jesus would pull me through. Before leaving the hospital, the biopsies revealed non-cancerous lung cancer, but the bone biopsies would be another two weeks before knowing those results.

The pet-scan revealed no bone cancer. I am facing kidney surgery in the coming months, but let me tell you about my

Jesus! He has met all my needs and He will pull me through because He strengthens me!

Anita Miller

Some things to think about:
- God will use your weakness to reveal His strength.
- Praising God in the midst of hard times can strengthen the faith of others.
- Your heavenly Father knows your needs.

How you can apply this to your life: When you praise God in your darkest hour, you encourage others to see God more clearly. Learning to trust God in your weakness will give you a better understanding of who God is and His desire to provide you with all that you need.

Digging deeper: Psalm 34:9-10 *Oh, fear the LORD, you his saints, for those who fear him have no lack! The young lions suffer want and hunger; but those who seek the LORD lack no good thing.*

How you can pray about this: Heavenly Father, help me to trust that You are all that I need for every situation. Thank You for walking with me through hard times and for taking my heavy burdens from me. Most of all, thank You for the unbelievable gift of Your Son, Jesus Who makes the Way for us to have eternal life with You!

Remember this: God supplies our every need!

My Redeemer Lives

For I know that my Redeemer lives, and at the last he will stand upon the earth. And after my skin has been thus destroyed, yet in my flesh I shall see God, whom I shall see for myself, and my eyes shall behold, and not another. My heart faints within me!
Job 19:25-27

When suffering enters our lives we cry out for relief. When relief does not come, we beg for an answer: why are we suffering? Are we being punished for some act of sin that we committed?

I know in whom I have believed, my Redeemer lives and all the plans and promises of God will be fully realized. Job knew what God said, God would perform.

He was unaware that the life he lived, the actions he took, the decision he made to trust would be used to encourage others that come after him.

If you're grateful for someone or something, you'll feel the need to appreciate them in one way or another. We often get so caught up with our everyday lives that it slips our mind to show kindness to others.

Robin Stapleton

Some things to think about:
- Sometimes it is hard to understand or accept our suffering.
- We can trust in the promises of God found in the Word of God.
- Often we don't realize how our actions and decisions can encourage those who come after us.

How you can apply this to your life: Our faith will be strengthened when we know and trust in the promises of God that He shares with us in the Bible. During times of suffering, it is good to be aware of how our actions can strengthen others.

Digging deeper: Joshua 21:45 *Not one word of all the good promises that the LORD had made to the house of Israel had failed; all came to pass.*

How you can pray about this: How amazing are You, God! How good are Your promises and how precious is Your Word! Thank You for how you care for us so perfectly. Lord Jesus, help us to rest on Your promises and trust You when we are suffering. Show us how to have faith like Job in every situation.

Remember this: Every promise of God is good!

Embrace The Struggle

Count it all joy, my brothers,
when you meet trials of various kinds,
for you know that the testing of your faith
produces steadfastness.
James 1:2-3

My name is Chris. I have been a heroin addict, drug dealer, and gang member. You name it and I did it. I spent 20 years of my adult life in bondage to the things of this world. It was when I was in prison for trafficking, that these verses really hit home.

I was raised in church. So, the things I was doing, I knew better. When I truly became a believer in Jesus Christ, I thought that everything would be easier. Boy was I wrong.

When the pandemic hit, I had earned my work-release. That was the ultimate goal for me. That would allow me more freedom, and an opportunity to have money saved up upon my release. The problem was God knew that I was not ready for that.

When some trouble hit the block, I tried to be a hero, tried to break up a brawl. That's when the other guy I tried to restrain hit the floor, his arm broke. He suffered a compound fracture. I got blamed for it. I was placed in segregation.

The administration board needed someone to hold responsible for the injury, that became me. I ended up spending the next 15 months in restrictive housing.

There went my minimum custody, work release, visits, phone calls. I lost everything I had worked so hard to achieve. It seemed there was absolutely no reason for this to be happening to me.

After all, I was a Christian. I was one of the good guys. That is where God showed me my complacency. He showed me how to have complete dependence on Him.

This is the time in my life I experienced the most growth, my spiritual maturity. God sat me down and dealt with me in ways that words can't describe. In a season that felt so alone and unfair, He was there with me, providing His strength.

Chris Cordero

Some things to think about:
- Becoming a Christian does not mean life will be easier
- Christians still struggle with sin
- God works so powerfully through your trials

How you can apply this to your life: Remember that it is through your trials that God strengthens and grows your faith. If you are a follower of Jesus, you will still struggle with sin and you will still have trials. Remember to turn to Christ in these times and allow Him to teach you a new way to live that honors God.

Digging deeper: Romans 5:3-4 *Not only that, but we rejoice in our sufferings, knowing that suffering produces endurance, and endurance produces character, and character produces hope,*

How you can pray about this: My sweet Lord, You always know what is needed in every situation for me to become more like You. I want to be more like You but this life is hard, sometimes and I am so weak! Please Lord Jesus, forgive me when I choose my sin over my relationship with You. Thank You for how You never give up on your children.

Remember this: When you completely depend on God instead of on your own self reliance, He will show you more of Himself and teach you how to be more like Him.

God's Law is Perfect

The Law of the Lord is perfect, converting the soul. The Testimony of the Lord is sure, making wise the simple.
Psalm 19:7

We often think of laws as burdens. And in human systems, they usually are. But God's laws are perfect, and He has given them to us not to weigh us down, but so that we may be renewed by them.

Love God, and love others. This is the summary of God's law. And as His law grows us in wisdom, we are renewed by venturing deeper into His love.

Jesus promises an easy yoke for us. But the one thing He asks for is commitment. Jesus wants us with Him wholeheartedly not longing for what we left to follow Him, and not wondering what could have been. Jesus calls us to serve Him with full surrender. And keep our eye on the prize ahead as we journey together with Him.

Jonah cried out to God from the belly of the fish. What a place for a prayer meeting! This should teach that there is no place on earth where we cannot or should not pray to God.

There is no situation we can be in where He will be unable to hear us and deliver us. Note that the Hebrew for "hell" can also be rendered "grave" in many cases. It was as if Jonah was dead and gone in the fish's belly was his tomb, but God heard him and brought him back.

David Grant

Some things to think about:
- God's law is perfect it is never a burden
- God uses His law to bring renewal
- God hears you no matter where you are

How you can apply this to your life: Spending time reading God's Word will change your life and your relationship with God. When you open up your Bible, you step into the presence of God. This is where God will often work to teach you and show you more of Himself.

Digging deeper: Psalm 1:1-2 *Blessed is the man who walks not in the counsel of the wicked, nor stands in the way of sinners, nor sits in the seat of scoffers; but his delight is in the law of the LORD, and on his law he meditates day and night.*

How you can pray about this: Lord, Your love knows no bounds. I thank You for giving me Your perfect law, which guides me in Your truth and centers me in Your love in every command and decree. Grow me in wisdom so that I may experience the full refreshment and renewal of Your love through Your commands. In Jesus' Name, Amen

Remember this: Be renewed by the Word of God!

Made Whole

Consequently, he is able to save to the uttermost those who draw near to God through him, since he always lives to make intercession for them.
Hebrews 7:25

Ever had this happen to you? You start something but you find you lack the tools necessary to complete the job or the strength and the ability to finish well?

As humans we sometimes find ourselves unable to change our situation, our circumstances, ourselves and the things we do. It causes anxiety, stress, feelings of hopelessness, and even anger. We hate to admit it, but there are some things we cannot do.

This verse speaks of God's ability to fully save, change, and transform a life. Christ's death on the cross made a way for us to come to God for forgiveness and salvation. Nothing we can ever do will save us; we will fall short of that every time.

We have to swallow our pride, confess our inability and humbly come to the cross. We come by the way of Christ's death, burial and resurrection.

Once this is done God isn't done with us. He then stands in the way of the enemy preventing him from bringing us to our knees. Christ fights for us, even praying for us, that's what it means by intercession. Imagine the God who created the universe, defeated death, hell and the grave is actively praying for you and me.

So hold your head up high, trusting in the work of salvation, complete and whole, able to save us completely and wonderfully. For what we lack as human beings, God more than makes up for it.

Doug Hall

Some things to think about:
- Christ's death on the cross makes a way for us to be saved
- Jesus can fully transform our lives
- We must come before Jesus in humility and repentance

How you can apply this to your life: Remember that Jesus has already done everything that God requires for you to be saved. We can never reach eternity with God by being good enough or working hard enough. Salvation is a free gift from God through Jesus. Let Jesus change your life today.

Digging deeper: Romans 8:34 *Who is to condemn? Christ Jesus is the one who died—more than that, who was raised—who is at the right hand of God, who indeed is interceding for us.*

How you can pray about this: Thank You Lord Jesus for the incredible gift of salvation! Thank you for interceding for us and calling us to Yourself. Help us to see our sins and realize that because of You we can be forgiven and we can live lives that honor and glorify You.

Remember this: Jesus is praying for us!

Where Do You Find Security?

God is our refuge and strength,
an ever present help in trouble.
Psalm 46:1

This verse tells us that God is our security. Where do you find security? Is it in worldly possessions, or is your security rooted in faith?

I have found myself stuck in so many troubling times that it's hard to list. I was so broken that I overdosed 6 times in a matter of a month. I felt as if there was nothing left in my life.

I had a spiritual awakening in 2018. I overdosed and died and this time I almost didn't make it back. I had an entire room of emergency responders trying to resuscitate me. While I was unconscious and not breathing, I witnessed God's awesome presence. I heard a voice only audible to myself. He said "Go back, all your pain will be over soon".

I felt a warm embrace in that place that I can't even describe. I literally had to die to embrace the life God has given me. I'm so grateful for that experience because it changed my life. Since that date I have focused only on following God's plan.

I learned a valued lesson in that disaster. God has a plan for all our lives. Any struggle that you go through is a lesson. It's meant to teach you not to hurt you, it's to provide growth or a change within. I had to learn my lessons the hardest of ways. It has provided so many blessings in my life.

I understand now that there is a reason for everything. I now seek my refuge in God. I allow him to lead and I follow instead of trying to lead myself aimlessly.

Ashley McPeters

Some things to think about:
- Is your sense of security found in the world or in your relationship with God?
- Our struggles are meant to teach us not to hurt us.
- Trust in God's plan, even when it is hard.

How you can apply this to your life: Be aware of how much the world is influencing you and make an effort to be more focussed on God's plan than on things of the world. Be aware of how God is using your struggles to change you from within.

Digging deeper: Proverbs 3:25-26 *Do not be afraid of sudden terror or of the ruin of the wicked, when it comes, for the LORD will be your confidence and will keep your foot from being caught.*

How you can pray about this: Father I am so thankful for how You take care of me and provide for me. I know that Your plan for me is for my good and that I can find complete security in You. Jesus, keep teaching me, I want to learn! I choose to follow You!

Remember this: God has a good plan for your life!

Through Him All Things Are Possible

Blessed are those who mourn, for they shall be comforted.
Blessed are the meek, for they shall inherit the earth.
Blessed are those who hunger and thirst for righteousness,
for they shall be satisfied. Blessed are the merciful, for they
shall receive mercy. Blessed are the pure in heart, for they
shall see God. Blessed are the peacemakers,
for they shall be called sons of God.
Blessed are those who are persecuted for righteousness'
sake, for theirs is the kingdom of heaven.
Matthew 5:4-6

You cannot mourn (Matthew 5:4) without appreciating how insufficient you are to handle life by your own strength. This was a concept that was completely out of my grasp.

I always thought that part of being a man was to "handle my own business". I could not let God work in my life until I got me out of the way.

You cannot be meek (Matthew 5:5) unless you have experienced and admitted a need for your gentleness. The world needs more loving and caring people. Accepting and showing kindness is the first step.

You cannot hunger and thirst for righteousness (Matthew 5:6) if you consider yourself already good.

Putting my pride aside and admitting to myself that I was broken and needed help allowed me to open myself to all the goodness God wanted to show me.

You cannot be merciful (Matthew 5:7) without recognizing your own need for mercy. We all need mercy and without it I would still be the same miserable human being I was all these years. Mercy is proof that God really does love me.

You cannot be pure in heart (Matthew 5:8) if your heart is filled with pride. Pride is a result of selfishness. I had to replace selfishness with selflessness.

You cannot be a peacemaker (Matthew 5:9) if you believe that you are always right. If you always have to be right then you will find yourself with the need to fight for that sense of rightness everytime. There is never gonna be any peace in that.

You cannot stand up for Christ in the face of persecution (Matthew 5:10) without putting Him before yourself. Putting Christ first in my life has given me the strength and confidence to stand for all that is right. Through Him ALL things are possible!!!

Jason Wallace

Some things to think about:
- You need God's strength to live this life
- You cannot live a life of thinking only about yourself and still be an effective servant to God and others.
- You are not good by nature but through God

How you can apply this to your life: It is good to remember that you cannot perform tasks for God without the strength of God. You must allow God's strength to work in you and through you. If you submit to God's plan and put aside your pride you will see God more clearly and have a deeper relationship with Him.

Digging deeper: 1 Peter 5:6-7 *Humble yourselves, therefore, under the mighty hand of God so that at the proper time he may exalt you, casting all your anxieties on him, because he cares for you.*

How you can pray about this: Father, I know that You are good and I am not. I admit that I try to take care of myself instead of submitting myself to Your care. Help me to put myself aside and allow You to be God of my life. I love You, Lord. Thank You for how You care for me!

Remember this: God's love for you never fails!

Christian Fellowship

not neglecting to meet together, as is the habit of some,
but encouraging one another, and all the more
as you see the Day drawing near.
Hebrews 10:25

This verse is a reminder of the importance of fellowship with other believers. It is easy to get caught up in our own lives and forget to connect with others, but this is a mistake. Fellowship is essential for our spiritual growth.

When we gather together with other believers, we are reminded of the truth of God's Word. We are encouraged by the testimonies of others, and we are strengthened in our faith. We also have the opportunity to serve one another and to grow in love.

The Bible tells us that we are not to neglect our meeting together. This means that we should make it a priority to attend church services and other gatherings of believers. We should also make time to connect with other believers in our community.

If you are not currently involved in a church or other Christian community, I encourage you to find one. Fellowship is essential for our spiritual growth and development.

As we grow in our faith, we will be more and more drawn to fellowship with other believers. We will find that our faith is strengthened and our lives are enriched when we connect with others who share our love for Jesus Christ.

Jim Smith

Some things to think about:
- God's Word is true
- Connecting with other believers strengthens our faith
- When we serve others we grow in love

How you can apply this to your life: When you find a church or community that you feel comfortable with, get involved! Attend services, join a small group, and serve in whatever capacity you can. Fellowship is a two-way street. We need to be willing to give and receive, to serve and be served.

Digging deeper: Matthew 18:20 "*For where two or three are gathered in my name, there am I among them.*"

How you can pray about this: Father, it is so amazing that You have provided us with a family of faith that we might encourage and strengthen each other in love. Help us to remember to treat each other just as You treat us. Show us how to forgive each other and how to serve and be served in strength and humility. Thank You Jesus for how You provide us with a perfect example of God's love for His people.

Remember this: Love others as Jesus loves you!

His Refuge

The LORD redeems the life of his servants; none of those who take refuge in him will be condemned.
Psalm 34:22

For me, this scripture is a refuge to a broken heart. When I cry out to the Lord, He always answers my cry. Sometimes I may be weak and hungry for something specific or sometimes I just seek His love.

With my past, I would always be running from God. I would run from the One who is truly calling for me. He is Who I need to be running to, yet my flesh is weak.

GOD TURN IT AROUND!!!

Throughout Psalm 34 God tells us that when we take refuge in Him, fear Him, and follow Him, then we will be delivered. When we seek Him with our whole heart we lack for nothing!

These words are such a comfort to me and strengthen me so much! That is why I will forever fear Him and lack nothing.

On my journey I've learned that while sometimes negative circumstances continue and God instead provides a different type of shelter and refuge from within the storm or war that rages on.

These verses in Psalm 34 are good for all of us and provide us with promises from God that we can all relate to in our lives. We can trust Him.

Kim Miller

Some things to think about:
- We can take refuge in God.
- God hears our cries and answers.
- When we seek after God and stand in awe of Who He is then we can be assured trust in His provision.

How you can apply this to your life: It is good for us to have a healthy fear of God for He is mighty indeed. He is able to do anything and He loves to take care of His children. When we seek Him and trust Him with all parts of our lives then we will see how He is working all around us.

Digging deeper: Psalm 91:1-2 *He who dwells in the shelter of the Most High will abide in the shadow of the Almighty. I will say to the LORD, "My refuge and my fortress, my God, in whom I trust." For he will deliver you from the snare of the fowler and from the deadly pestilence.*

How you can pray about this: God, today we seek to grow closer to You in all parts of our lives. We know that You are our perfect refuge from the storms of this life and we need Your provision and protection every day! Help us to be more aware of Your presence in our lives. Thank You, Lord, for all that you are and all that You do.

Remember this: He WILL deliver you!

God's Provision

Trust in the Lord with all your heart and lean not unto your own understanding; in all thy ways acknowledge Him and He will make your paths straight.

Proverbs 3:5-8

Have you ever truly laid your storm or chaos at His feet? Do you know that you have a choice to trust Him? You are not alone, and God, your Heavenly Father, will never leave you or forsake you (Hebrews 13:5).

He is always there waiting for you to give Him your storm so he can take what was meant for evil and turn it to your good (Genesis 50:20). God loves you and wants to meet you where you are, especially in the middle of your storm.

Many years ago, my family was facing the possibility of being homeless. There was nothing available to rent and we were trying to buy a used mobile home. We had two young children and the thought of them without a place to sleep or call home was unbearable. We couldn't fix this, only God could.

I remembered something our Pastor once said "Trust God with your worst scenario and watch what He does with it". I was so overwhelmed with the weight I was carrying, the guilt and shame of not having a home. I fell on my knees and began pouring my heart out to God. I cried and gave all of it to Him.

That Monday I was reminded of the phrase *"you have not because you ask not"*. I wanted a home that is safe and decent with a room for each child and a place for their belongings and a bathroom. We would make do so they could have what they needed. We had been waiting to hear about a repossessed trailer for sale. We barely had enough for a down payment.

On Thursday we received a call saying to come to their office. We were scared and trusting God. When we arrived, we were told that the original trailer was sold. Then the manager said but we have another one available for half the price and twice as nice that will work with your down payment.

It has three bedrooms, two bathrooms, and even a garden tub. It is brand new and barely used. I almost fainted. We walked through and signed the papers before they could change their minds. The manager said "I just need to know where to deliver this."

My Father-in-Law said "right next door to our home". He had secretly cleared a piece of their property and had everything ready for our new home, because he knew God would provide. He had told us that he was clearing it for his new workshop.

I cried all the way home. We still had to figure out where we were going to stay that weekend. Our landlord came over on Friday and said she would give us enough time to move because the new renters weren't able to move in yet.

I grew up as a military kid where you were always struggling to make ends meet and living in different countries. I always felt like I didn't have a sense of "home" outside of my actual family. I had never owned a piece of land or a home.

God blessed us with both. I could grow a garden and provide for my kids if needed. I had extended family that were close by, we could visit and make memories every day. This was my secret prayer for my family all along. God heard my cries and He met me where my heart was.

Not only did He meet our needs He gave us His heart's desire for us, because I was willing to have a real conversation with my Father. He met His daughter in her lowest point and loved her through it because she trusted Him with her heart. Just trust Him once and see what happens. I'm thankful God has my heart and that He will always be there to help if I just trust Him.

Karen MacKinnon

Some things to think about:
- Have you ever experienced provision that could only come from God?
- Do you ask God for what you really want and trust Him to provide?
- God meets us where we are and walks us through

How you can apply this to your life: Trust God and believe that He is able to provide over and above all that you can imagine. Ask God for what you want and have faith that He will provide for you in His great mercy. Talk to God plainly and truthfully about your needs and your heart, He wants to hear from you.

Digging deeper: Ephesians 3:20 *Now to him who is able to do far more abundantly than all that we ask or think, according to the power at work within us,*

How you can pray about this: Thank You, Father, for how You know our every need and provide more than we can even imagine. Thank You for how You love us and desire to show us Your heart in our difficult times. Help us to always share Your love with others.

Remember this: There is nothing that can put limits on God.

Fearless

Have I not commanded you? Be strong and courageous.
Do not be frightened, and do not be dismayed,
for the LORD your God is with you wherever you go.
Joshua 1:9

Are you fearful about the future? Maybe it's something going on in your life today that has you afraid. Are you worried you may have to handle the situation all alone? I know I have felt this way more than once in my life, but I have great news for you!

God tells us in Joshua 1:9 *"Have I not commanded you? Be strong and courageous. Do not be afraid or dismayed, for the Lord your God is with you wherever you go."* What a promise from the Father that whatever tomorrow brings we don't have to face it alone!

During my time in prison my mind was a mess thinking about the uncertainty of the future, and what it looked like for me. There were times I was afraid and would worry myself to death.

Was I going to complete my parole? Would I truly be able to live this new life in recovery, even when the temptations come? Will I be able to find a job to support my family as a convicted felon?

Philippians 4:13 tells us *"I can do all things because of Christ who strengthens me"*. There's nothing we can't accomplish when Christ is the center of our life. There are no obstacles we can't overcome and no uncertainties that should leave us stricken with fear.

We serve a God that will carry us through anything. We may not always know what the future holds, but we know Who

44

holds the future. Through Christ we can live fearlessly! Choose today to trust Him with your whole life. He won't ever let you down.

Robert McNeely

Some things to think about:
- With God, we never face things alone.
- God tells us not to be afraid but to be strong and courageous
- We can do all things through Christ, He gives us strength

How you can apply this to your life: Seek to find calmness and peace in God and not in the world. Let God strengthen you and calm your fears through His Word and through prayer. During times of fear, seek out godly counsel from strong Christian friends who love Jesus and trust in His Word.

Digging deeper: John 14:27 *Peace I leave with you; my peace I give to you. Not as the world gives do I give to you. Let not your hearts be troubled, neither let them be afraid.*

How you can pray about this: Father, I know that You are in control and that I do not need to fear, but that is so hard to do sometimes! It is hard to give up these fears and worries when the world is such a confusing and chaotic place. Thank You for telling us so often in Your Word that we do not need to fear but that we can have peace from You and rest in Your promises.

Remember this: Through Christ we can live fearlessly!

Keeping Our Eyes On Him

And the Lord said, "My presence will go with you,
and I will give you rest"
Exodus 33:14

It's very interesting to read the above verse and be encouraged from this promise and from this truth, but I believe we should look a little deeper. I would encourage you to read the verses leading up to it as well.

The Israelites had quite recently been freed from over 400 years of slavery and had been given the opportunity to live in the 'Promised land'. Along their journey to this land and in just a short period of time, the newly freed children of God began to take their eyes off of Him and started placing their trust in their own understanding.

They were believing what their eyes were seeing. Things were not as they had imagined. They found themselves consumed by worry, stress and even anger because of the seemingly dire circumstances surrounding them. They were without a physical home, yet they were being led by God both day and night as to where to camp. They had no food, but every morning God gave them manna from heaven for their physical sustenance.

Although they were now free from the bondage of slavery, they had already become frustrated with God because they neither trusted nor approved of His plan for them. It was not only insufficient for them, but also inconsistent with their perceptions of what their new life in freedom should be like. God's ways simply did not align with the thoughts and desires of their worldly hearts and minds.

During this time, God's servant, Moses, did not take his eyes off of God nor did he allow his faith to waiver. In fact, he walked and communicated relentlessly with God, and it pleased the Lord. God then offered grace and mercy to literally millions, based on the actions and faith of one.

Anthony Collins

Some things to think about:
- Keeping our hearts set on God helps us to live in closer relationship with Him.
- God provides all that we need and we can trust His perfect provision
- Remember that Jesus' work on the cross was enough to cover anything we face.

How you can apply this to your life: As we grow in our walk with God we will learn to examine our hearts and lives and to recognize when we are not keeping our eyes on Him. It is easy to be distracted by the world and we must be ever aware of how the world tries to distract us from Jesus.

Digging deeper: Colossians 3:1-3 *If then you have been raised with Christ, seek the things that are above, where Christ is, seated at the right hand of God. Set your minds on things that are above, not on things that are on earth. For you have died, and your life is hidden with Christ in God.*

How you can pray about this: Thank you, Abba, for how You take care of us! Teach us to always keep our eyes on You. Forgive us, Lord, when we allow the things of this world to distract us from our walk with You, Jesus.

Remember this: You are no longer a slave, but you are now free through Jesus!

God Gives A new Thing

See, I am doing a new thing! Now it springs up; do you not perceive it? I am making a way in the wilderness and streams in the wasteland.
Isaiah 43:19

In this passage God is telling us to look for or at something. There is something that He wants us to see, or He wants us to know is there. He wants to show us something. What a wonderful thing.

Our Heavenly Father, the Creator of the universe, the world, the giver of all good, our Maker and the one who calls us friend, wants our attention to show us something. At a time like this we have often taken our attention and maybe even our affection off of the Father and have begun looking at distractions that will bring us no good.

The Lord wants to show us the new thing that He is doing in our life. There are seasons in our life. Every season has something new in it. The new season is springing up. It is happening right before our eyes.

God asks us: *"do you not perceive it?"* The definition of "perceive" is to become aware of or conscious of something. The question is are we staying close to our Father so we can be aware of what He is saying and doing? Are we listening to Him continually and maintaining a relationship with Him?

It's in these places in life God wants to make a way specifically for you. He has a path that is designed only with you in mind. So, don't give up, be aware that our Father is doing a new thing in your life!

Kimberly Wilkerson

Some things to think about:
- The God of the universe wants to show you a new thing
- Do you seek to see what God is doing in your life?
- How important is it to you to seek and maintain a strong and close relationship with God?

How you can apply this to your life: It is good for you to seek to see what God is doing in your life. Reading God's Word and allowing God to speak into your life through scripture as well as through solid biblical teaching can help you to see the "new thing" that he is doing.

Digging deeper: 2 Corinthians 5:17 *Therefore, if anyone is in Christ, he is a new creation. The old has passed away; behold, the new has come.*

How you can pray about this: Lord help me to see this new thing that You are doing! Thank You for how You want to show me what You are doing and that You have an amazing and good plan for my life. Help me, Father, to stay close to You and to do all that I can to maintain this beautiful relationship with You.

Remember this: Don't give up! God has an amazing plan designed just for you!

Healing

Behold, I will bring to it health and healing,
and I will heal them and reveal to them
abundance of prosperity and security.
Jeremiah 33:6

My name is Julie McAllister and I have six years of sobriety. For over twenty years I lived a life of chaos. My childhood wasn't the best and I couldn't wait til I was eighteen and could leave. I used to yell that, in my teens, at my parents.

Even as a child I had so much hate in me. Abused mentally, physically and sexually I was filled with rage and bitterness. I hated myself. I never felt like I was enough, just me. I used food, sex, manipulation, anything I could to get the attention I needed to feel loved. And it never ended well.

By 2016 there had been four overdoses at my house. Two of them were my son. I had walked both my children into that life by what they had watched us do for years, and here I was breathing life into one of them. Not once but twice.

One day I remember looking up to the skies crying and saying "you've taken it all please don't take the only three things I have left, my husband and my two sons".

Within six months they had left me too. I was broken and at my lowest in life. I cried every time I opened my mouth to talk.

I came to Marion and met the people at Freedom Life. That was May 2017 and I've been with them since. They are like family to me, and God has given my boys back to me and they too are clean and sober.

God changed that!! He placed the right people in my path to help save me and my boys!!

Even after my second divorce I have peace and I know that with God I can do anything I set out to do. I have a beautiful home and a wonderful job. And my boys have their own little families that I get to be a part of!! That's love!!

I love myself now, I'm no longer searching because LOVE found me!!!! GOD IS LOVE! I AM HEALED! HIS PROMISES ARE FAITHFUL!!! He can heal you too!!!

Julie McAllister

Some things to think about:
- No matter how far you have moved away from God, He is close to you
- There is nothing that God cannot overcome
- God's love can always find you and heal you if you call on Him.

How you can apply this to your life: Reach out to God no matter what your situation may be. He is ready and wants to bring healing and comfort to all those who will seek Him and believe.

Digging deeper: Psalm 107:19-21 *Then they cried to the LORD in their trouble, and he delivered them from their distress. He sent out his word and healed them, and delivered them from their destruction. Let them thank the LORD for his steadfast love, for his wondrous works to the children of man!*

How you can pray about this: Jesus, I am so grateful that You are always willing to meet me wherever I am and wash me clean again! Thank You for how You are never far away from us and that whenever we seek You with our whole heart we will find You.

Remember this: God's mercies are new every morning!

Practicing Gratitude

But to all who did receive him,
who believed in his name,
he gave the right to become children of God,
John 1:12

Gratitude can have a long lasting effect on a person's life. When you develop negative thought patterns it can change your outlook on the world in a different way. It can cause you to have a more difficult life and cause more thoughts that trigger unhealthy responses.

The best way to overcome bad thoughts is to practice gratitude. A family member leaves the Lord and goes into sin. This can rip our hearts apart. Often, God does not explain to us why our hearts are broken and in so much pain. He wants us to seek Him in difficult times. We must find a place of gratitude and trust toward our Creator.

How does God exist if He is allowing people to fail and leave His faith? In the real world bad things can happen to good people and how we respond to these times can be the difference between hope and despair. God wants us to have hope in Him, He wants our hearts to know Him and respond to Him.

"With God all things are possible" In other words, God is on my side, I can accomplish anything I want to do. We claim God's power that gives us the ability to chase any dream we want.

Robin Stapleton

Some things to think about:
- When we learn to be more grateful, our lives can be more hopeful and healthy
- It is hard to understand why bad things happen and why God allows pain
- It is important to remember that God is always in control

How you can apply this to your life: If we can fill our hearts and minds with the truth of God's Word and if we can seek to be more grateful for how God loves and cares for us, then we can have more hope and trust in His plan for us. Remember that nothing is impossible for God and that He has a good plan for our lives and promises to be with us always when we believe in Him.

Digging deeper: Hebrews 10:23 *Let us hold fast the confession of our hope without wavering, for he who promised is faithful.*

How you can pray about this: Lord Jesus, we want to believe that You plan everything for our good, but when times are hard, we struggle to see Your goodness. We believe Your promises and know that You can do anything, but sometimes we have doubts especially when we are hurting or being hurt by others. Help us, Lord, to see You in all of our circumstances! Help us to have grateful hearts for You, Jesus, and for all that You have done to provide for our salvation and eternal life with You.

Remember this: Nothing is impossible for God, He cannot be defeated!

There is Hope

The sovereign Lord is my strength! He makes me surefooted as deer, able to tread upon the heights.
Habakkuk 3:19

The spirit of the living God is upon us. Whom shall I fear? Nothing but the love of Jesus. The Lord is my strength and my salvation, I give all my heart to him. Where does our strength come from? God. We are weak but He is strong.

We are nothing without the help from our Savior. He gives us exactly what we need when we need it. The problem is that we get so far ahead of His plan that we can't even see. We are in the habit of making plans, seeking out our own agenda, and that usually gets us every single time.

Our Lord will make us what He wants us to be, we don't have to do anything. It may seem hard at the time when we are in it and it feels as if God is being too hard on us, guess what, He has to. If life was easy, we would all be in a world of mess.

Are you in trouble? Hurt? No way out? There is a way out, every single time there is a way out of our mess. Freedom Life knows all about getting people out of their mess. Life gets in the way and sometimes there seems like there is no way out. Yes, we all get in over our head, there is refuge and hope.

Hope is a Freedom Life family that extends love, honesty, and truth through God's word. There is hope, hope for the hopeless. Hope for a future, hope for a better life. Do we have all the answers? No we do not. Do we need all the answers? Absolutely not.

God gives us what we need and in the time that we need it. The answers are all right there in black and white, the Bible.

Kim Brown

Some things to think about:
- Where does your strength come from?
- Remember that God will guide our steps and if we just stop controlling things and submit to His plan
- There is hope, we can trust in that, God provides all that we need when we need it.

How you can apply this to your life: We must first believe in Jesus and His promise that He will take care of us and remain near to us. When we have struggles, and He says we will, then we seek to be closer to Him and allow Him to take care of our mess. There is a way out, through belief in the truth of who Jesus is and what He has done for us.

Digging deeper: Ephesians 1:18 *having the eyes of your hearts enlightened, that you may know what is the hope to which he has called you, what are the riches of his glorious inheritance in the saints,*

How you can pray about this: Lord, You are enough! All that we need! We know that You have the answers to every situation we face if we will just turn to You and trust You to care for us. Jesus, save us from ourselves, help us to clearly see how You are waiting for us to seek and trust You in every part of our lives. Thank You for being patient with us, Lord.

Remember this: There is hope for the hopeless and freedom for the future, through our Savior, Jesus Christ.

God Works in Suffering

Through him we have also obtained access by faith into this grace in which we stand, and we rejoice in hope of the glory of God. Not only that, but we rejoice in our sufferings, knowing that suffering produces endurance, and endurance produces character, and character produces hope, and hope does not put us to shame, because
God's love has been poured into our hearts through the Holy Spirit who has been given to us.
Romans 5:2-5

It is often easy for us to see God at work when we are experiencing joy and when we hear others talk about how God has blessed them or how He is working in their lives. This is the space we want to dwell in, isn't it? It is easy and comfortable and we could just pull up a chair and watch God's glory unfold forever.

But what about when you are going through struggles? When someone you love is suffering. When you don't feel blessed or can't see how God is possibly at work in a devastating situation.

Read Romans 5:2-5. Just read it! I will give you a little taste. If you are a believer: you have been declared righteous, you have peace, you have access to God, you can rejoice in the hope of glory, you can rejoice in afflictions because God uses hard times to produce endurance which builds character and brings hope. There is so much more in this chapter about Jesus and His sacrifice for us, about reconciliation and God's grace.

The Spirit of Jesus has poured His love into your heart and He continues to live there to be your Comforter and Teacher. He does not leave you, EVER. If you are truly saved then He lives IN you and you are never in any situation where He is not there.

Recently, I have experienced some scary and truly devastating situations as well as some very difficult losses. When things were at their worst, I felt like I was in such a heavy dark place that I could not see how God was doing anything, and yet He was not only doing something, He was purposefully orchestrating every minute detail of the situation. It took a minute for me to see it because I was distracted by so much craziness but He was there and He was working.

God strengthened my faith and He showed me so much love and encouragement through scripture, prayer, and people all around me. Why did it take me so long to look for it? How many times in my past have I missed this opportunity? I don't know the answer to those questions and honestly, I don't really care that much anymore.

Once you learn to see where God is at work, and you feel His presence in your struggles, it becomes hard to look away. Now what I seek is Him. Wherever He is working, whatever He is doing, even when it is hard and messy, that is exactly where I want to be. When you finally submit to His Spirit inside you, you'll know this too and then everything changes.

Janis Bolick

Some things to think about:
- God is working in our lives when we suffer just as He works when we rejoice.
- Our suffering is used by God to teach us endurance and mature our faith.
- God is in control of every situation, we are not.

How you can apply this to your life: There is so much hope that can be found in reading God's Word! When we seek to come into God's presence and hear from Him through scripture, we have every opportunity to know Him better and to see His great power and strength. Seek God in all areas of your life and you will see Him and know Him like never before.

Digging deeper: 2 Corinthians 4:16-17 *So we do not lose heart. Though our outer self is wasting away, our inner self is being renewed day by day. For this light momentary affliction is preparing for us an eternal weight of glory beyond all comparison,*

How you can pray about this: Oh Father, how we long to be closer to You! We are so broken and we so easily get caught up in our flesh, help us! We need guidance from Your Spirit to comfort us and show us how to glorify You in our suffering. We remember how Jesus suffered and we know that He did that so we could belong to You, Lord! Such a gift! Help us to never forget what had to be done to redeem our broken lives and bring us to You.

Remember this: God will use every situation in your life to grow you and stretch you and draw you closer to Himself.

You Have a Voice

Whether you turn to the right or the left,
your ears will hear a voice behind you, saying,
"This is the way, walk in it."
Isaiah 30:21

I remember getting a call from Melissa of Freedom Life Ministries one evening inviting me to lunch the next day. At the time I wasn't sure why she called and wanted to meet with me. We knew each other because I had folks that attended Celebrate Recovery that were also clients of Freedom Life.

I asked her why she called and I was floored when she asked me to join the Freedom Life team as the Second Chance Act (SCA) Program Director.

I met with Danny and Melissa the following week. I accepted the position because I felt God leading me to serve as the SCA Program Director and wanted me to walk this path.

I look back at my past job experience and understand that God was training me to help those who really want help in getting their lives on track and walking closer with Him.

One of the unique things I have learned is that our clients have a voice with those who are still struggling to understand their value in connection to God and how much He loves them.

I am honored to be a part of the healing process in their lives and that God trusts me with it. I am thankful that I heard God say, "this is the way, walk in it"! I have found a family through those I work with and with those I serve as clients.

God loves each of us and can take our mistakes and bring good out of them. He created each of us for a purpose.

Melissa Marlowe

Some things to think about:
- We can look back and see how God has been working in our lives.
- Sharing your experiences can mean so much to others who are suffering
- God will use every bit of your suffering to help others through you if you will just be willing to share

How you can apply this to your life: Remember that you are loved by God, no matter what your circumstances are. When you share your experiences with others, it helps others to have hope and to be encouraged about their future. As you are reading this, please know that you are loved! You are not forgotten. God loves You!

Digging deeper: Romans 8:28 *And we know that for those who love God all things work together for good, for those called according to his purpose.*

How you can pray about this: Thank You, Father for how You love us and take care of us! We often overlook all that You do for us and how You protect us and provide the perfect path to serving You and those You want to reach. Help us to always be mindful of how You are at work in our lives.

Remember this: There is nothing God can't heal in your life!

What are you Carrying?

Praise be to the Lord, to God our Savior,
who daily bears our burdens.
Psalm 68:19

Burden simply means a heavy load. We all carry something. The problem is most of the stuff we carry, God never intended for us to carry. Think about the burdens you are carrying.

Over the years I have had the opportunity to lead a Christian Wilderness Camp. Here we take young people out backpacking to experience the wilderness. We give these young people very specific instructions on what they should carry when they go on these trips.

Even though we tell them what to pack, many pack way more stuff then they need. This leads to their fatigue even to the point that I have had to carry their packs at times.

Often, we become tired in this life because we don't know how to let others help us. Maybe you are there right now.

You're tired, you're worn out not so much because of the situations you have faced but rather how you have carried those so long in your life.

What are you carrying in your life right now that you need to give up? Is it a past hurt or sin? Why not let Jesus carry it for you?He is more than willing to carry your burdens, if you will just give them to Him.

Paul Cole

Some things to think about:
- Are you carrying burdens that you could be giving to God?
- Do you truly believe that God **wants** to carry your burdens for you?
- What keeps you from letting go of your burdens?

How you can apply this to your life: We all have the opportunity to allow Jesus to share our burdens, if we believe. He tells us that He is able to remove those things that weigh us down and give us rest. It is important to really believe what Jesus says in His Word about caring for us and loving us. It is not that only parts of the Bible is true but ALL of the Bible is true and we have the opportunity to be free of so much that weighs us down when we believe what God says.

Digging deeper: Matthew 11:28-30 *"Come to me, all who labor and are heavy laden, and I will give you rest. Take my yoke upon you, and learn from me, for I am gentle and lowly in heart, and you will find rest for your souls. For my yoke is easy, and my burden is light."*

How you can pray about this: Lord Jesus, it is so amazing that You would want to take our burdens from us and to free us from our past. We struggle to believe this because we feel so ashamed and burdened by our past sin. We love You and we desperately want to be free, help us to truly believe that You love us enough to remove all of these burdens.

Remember this: Drop your past and let the Lord carry it! What are you willing to give to Him today?

Blessed

For he will hide me in his shelter in the day of trouble;
he will conceal me under the cover of his tent;
he will lift me high upon a rock.
Psalms 27:5

I was in active addiction and living in my van for over a year. I finally went to the Friendship Home and then to an alcohol and drug treatment center which was supposed to be fourteen days, but my roommate had Covid 19 and I ended up staying for thirty-five days. It was during this time that I asked Jesus into my heart and my life changed forever. I went to Grace Home in Santee, SC for two months, but because of health problems I returned to the Friendship Home, a totally new creation in Jesus Christ!

I went back to the Friendship Home and worked on a program there. I participated in Cognitive Behavior Instruction (CBI) classes through Freedom Life Ministries and attended their weekly women's group.

Being back at the Friendship Home also allowed me the opportunity to reunite and work on my relationship with my daughter and grandchildren. I was allowed to help her get back and forth to work and watch my grandchildren. All things that were never a part of my world in active addiction.

Soon I was in my own apartment. My faith was strengthening. I was about four miles from my daughter. As I write this, I am now moving right beside my daughter. God worked out a reality in my life that I thought was only a dream. I am experiencing some health issues and being right beside my daughter brings comfort but also allows me to have my own space.

I have a church family, but also my Freedom Life family. God has blessed me beyond anything I could ever imagine. Even though I am facing an upcoming surgery, I know that my Jesus has me and will provide for me! He is faithful to His word in proving a shelter under his wings and a dwelling of my own! Let me tell you about my Jesus!

Anita Miller

Some things to think about:
- God is always in control of our circumstances
- God wants us to be redeemed if we will only trust Him
- God will provide all that we need for every situation

How you can apply this to your life: In difficult circumstances, we can often see God working and it is important to allow Him to work things out in His perfect will. Remember that sometimes we are to just be still in our situation and wait for our loving Father to work all the details out for us. These are the times when we learn to trust God.

Digging deeper: Psalm 27:14 *Wait for the LORD; be strong, and let your heart take courage; wait for the LORD!*

How you can pray about this: Father, thank You for how You provide for all of our situations. It is amazing to know that we can trust You no matter what happens in our circumstances. Help us to always remember how you are with us. Show us how we can trust you with every part of our lives.

Remember this: God provides perfectly for us in every situation and we only need to trust Him, He will do the rest!

God's Redemption and Love for His Children (that's us!)

And I will cleanse them from all their iniquity, whereby they have sinned against me; and I will pardon all their iniquities, whereby they have sinned, and whereby they have transgressed against me.
Jeremiah 33:8

I believe this verse reveals the true nature of God, to redeem, and not to condemn. You can see in the verse, the repetition of the forms of the words, iniquity, sin, and transgression. While there was much sin in the camp, God's grace and mercy was the plan to redeem Israel back to himself and was also the result of His perfect Love that He always has for his children.

This is the same love, sourced from the Father, that compelled Christ to walk the horrific path to Calvary, to give himself as our sacrifice, and to forever redeem lost mankind back to God. The Love that I speak of here is nothing like the worldly definition that most understand love to be.

Take a few quiet minutes and attempt to close out the rest of the world, and consider what Christ did for us, for you! His love for us is the only thing that could compel him to do so. Let's ask God to open our eyes to this kind of Love in which we certainly struggle to understand and to even comprehend.

God desires to share this love with us. Let's ask Him to open our hearts to the possibility of truly loving those closest to us and those farthest from us, unconditionally just as Christ did for each of us on the cross!

Anthony Collins

Some things to think about:
- God does not ever condemn His children
- Because of the cross, we can know that we are redeemed and loved by God
- God's love for us is beyond anything we can even understand

How you can apply this to your life: Take time to appreciate the sacrifice that Jesus made on the cross for you. Consider the depth of God's love for you in making this sacrifice. Practice living each day in the knowledge of how much God loves you.

Digging deeper: Romans 5:8 *but God shows his love for us in that while we were still sinners, Christ died for us.*

How you can pray about this: Jesus, we can never truly know the extent of Your love for us, but how grateful we are to have that love! Thank You for the incredible sacrifice You made for us and help us to remember how You love us especially when we are suffering. Teach us how to love others in the same way that You love us.

Remember this: Christ has already paid the ultimate price for you to live with Him in eternity. That is how much He loves you!

Rescued!

The Lord will save me, and we will sing with string instruments all the days of our lives in the temple of the Lord.
Isaiah 38:20

"The Lord will save me," that statement says so much to me. The Lord has saved me personally in so many ways. It's hard to comprehend the omnipotent power of the Lord. He has taken me out of the wreckage of addiction and saved me. In my active addiction I had absolutely nothing. I had no real friends to call on. I had no home and was estranged from my children and family. I was surrounded by people that wanted my company only for the drugs in my pocket.

I remember waking from some of my drug stupors to discover I had been robbed by the people I trusted to be around me. That life isn't a life I would recommend for anyone. It turned out to be a beautiful disaster because the Lord saved me from all of that.

Even when I literally died, he brought me back to life. Being surrounded by His presence was an experience that I will never forget. He opened my eyes and gave my life purpose. He has let me see everything He has saved me from. Everything I lost in addiction has been restored to me in abundance.

He restored me to sanity and health. He gave me fellowship in Christ and a new family to hold me accountable. The Lord heals me daily, I can feel His presence all around me. He has highlighted traumatic memories from my youth. He's granted me an opportunity to heal from all my brokenness.

God has rescued me so many times that I now, like the Psalmist, praise Him every day. I wake praising His name and go to sleep praising Him. I wake up happy and singing. He saved me from death and granted me life in abundance. He continues working on me and is always by my side and He won't leave yours either. All I needed to do was let him in. Invite Him in today.

Ashley McPeters

Some things to think about:
- The Lord will save you and restore you
- Trust God more and He will guide you
- Through salvation, provided by Jesus to every believer, God will restore each of us

How you can apply this to your life: God wants you to be healed and restored completely. He can make all things new and make you a completely new creation if you will invite Him into your life and trust in His Son, Jesus.

Digging deeper: John 1:12-13 *But to all who did receive him, who believed in his name, he gave the right to become children of God, who were born, not of blood nor of the will of the flesh nor of the will of man, but of God.*

How you can pray about this: God I want to trust in You and I want to be made into a new creation! I know that it is only through Jesus that I can be saved, help me to believe. Show me Yourself and teach me how I can come to know You better.

Remember this: Jesus restores me and makes me new!

What About Works?

But someone will say, "You have faith and I have works."
Show me your faith apart from your works,
and I will show you my faith by my works. You believe that
God is one; you do well. Even the demons believe—and
shudder! Do you want to be shown, you foolish person, that
faith apart from works is useless?
James 2:18-20

When I was young, I was taught that all you must do is say a prayer and you are going to Heaven. Yes, that is the start of the journey, but there is way more to it than that.

I said my prayer, but in my heart, I did not have true faith. I came to realize that when I was serving 70-90 months (about seven and a half years) in a North Carolina state prison for trafficking opiates.

I grew up in church. I played drums in the worship band, but I was still gambling, cussing, smoking, just living a life of sin. Even though in my self-righteous ways I thought I was doing good. I was not being obedient in any way at all. I had a very selfish spirit. It was all about what God could do for me.

I didn't understand why I had no peace, why God didn't care about my needs, which were actually wants. Well, through various circumstances, beyond my control, God got my attention. He brought me to James 2:18-20. There was so much confusion that set in.

Like I said, I was always taught that all you had to do was SAY that you believe. I went down to my knees; I asked God to give me clarity. And He did! It was so clear, the faith that I had was not from my heart. It was not genuine saving faith. I came to realize that I had spoken the sinner's prayer without actually understanding the true meaning. That our faith must be true faith.

True faith takes over and produces real, genuine change, deep within our hearts and soul. When we obtain faith like that, our actions will follow. The actions in our life, which are our works, will begin to align with the Word. We will have peace that comes over us.

The Bible says, *"For a good tree does not bear bad fruit, nor does a bad tree bear good fruit."* (Luke 6:43) When I really began analyzing this, I realized I had no fruit, no good works. It all started making sense to me. I wanted God to do things for me, but I didn't want to give Him anything in return. So, when I truly repented, I asked Him to come into my heart, for real this time.

My life changed. Yes, I was still locked up, with a lot of time to go, but my outlook on things changed, my works changed. It was evident in my life that I was now a true follower of Christ. Remember the demons believe but have no good work. We must have more faith than the demons. Faith without WORKS is DEAD

Chris Cordero

Some things to think about:
- True faith changes your heart
- When your heart is truly changed you will live differently
- God knows your heart and the truth about your faith

How you can apply this to your life: When you choose to believe and put your trust in Jesus as your Savior, you will be truly changed. Don't be fooled by worldly promises, trust in the promises of God to protect you and sustain you. True salvation will be obvious and it will change how you interact with others. It changes your heart.

Digging deeper: Ephesians 2:8-10 *For by grace you have been saved through faith. And this is not your own doing; it is the gift of God, not a result of works, so that no one may boast. For we are his workmanship, created in Christ Jesus for good works, which God prepared beforehand, that we should walk in them.*

How you can pray about this: Father, You know the truth that is in my heart. I need You so much! You have told me in Your Word that I am saved by grace and not by my works. I want to accept Your beautiful gift of salvation and I also want to serve others and live my life in a way that glorifies You. Teach me, Lord, in how I should live so that I can bear good fruit.

Remember this: Good works will come naturally when you have true faith and you are saved by grace.

Looking Forward

And the ransomed of the LORD shall return and come to
Zion with singing; everlasting joy shall be upon their heads;
they shall obtain gladness and joy,
and sorrow and sighing shall flee away.
Isaiah 51:11

One of my favorite movies is "Back to the Future." I remember watching and thinking how cool it was to see someone's idea of what the future would look like. Seeing the cars that floated in the sky, flying hoverboards, shoes that laced up and tied themselves, it painted a good picture of what the future would be like.

The people described in this verse, in this future, are people who have been saved by the grace of God. Redemption means something purchased that was sold, or lost, resulting in a transformation and a drastic change in life.

 A day is coming when God's children will all come to one place at one time together in Israel, Mount Zion. Think of it as the only church in a city the size of Los Angeles.

Look at what they will be doing, singing or worshiping as we would call it. Excited to be home, called to experience lasting joy. Today every emotion we have lasts only for a short while. In the future to come for God's children, (those who have asked Christ to forgive their sins and accepted Him as Lord and Savior), will never lose their joy again.

Experiencing a gladness that can never be taken away or lost because of circumstances beyond our control, where sorrow is never felt again. Now that's a future I can hardly wait to become a reality, and the great thing is; that what God says will happen, does happen.

Doug Hall

Some things to think about:
- Our salvation is a gift from God
- Our future, as believers, is full of joy
- God's promises for our future cannot ever fail

How you can apply this to your life: Remember that God has promised that His children will spend eternity with Him in heaven. As you go about your daily life, remember these promises and share the joy of your relationship with Jesus with others.

Digging deeper: Psalm 16:11 *You make known to me the path of life; in your presence there is fullness of joy; at your right hand are pleasures forevermore.*

How you can pray about this: Lord, thank You that You provide such an amazing and joyful future for us! Help us to walk closely with You today and to show others how You love and care for Your children. Give us courage and boldness to tell others about your love and Your plan for our future with You.

Remember this: Our future with Jesus is forever full of joy!

Wonderful Invitation

In nothing be anxious; but in everything by prayer and supplication with thanksgiving let your requests be made known to God.
Philippians 4:6

Anxious is sometimes a misunderstood word. Some think of it as being extremely excited when in fact the dictionary depicts it as experiencing worry, unease, or nervousness about something. Being anxious is usually the thoughts of an uncertain outcome which continues to replay in your mind.

God does not want us to experience these types of emotions and thoughts. He wants us at ease and in a state of certainty. In fact, this entire scripture is pointing us to the fact that God, our Heavenly Father, is directing us to trust Him. His desire is to commune with us. This is a sweet invitation to having a relationship with the Father. You might say a daily talk and walk with Him.

Everyday there are issues that we face. Maybe there's nothing as alarming as a dramatic issue on a daily basis but even the agenda for a normal day, or what needs to be done throughout a day, God would like for you to speak with Him about it.

Kinda like us asking Him, "What do you have in mind for the day Lord?" and Him asking us, "What are your cares and concerns for the day my child?" We should talk it over with Him.

Sometimes we let things get bottled up inside because we haven't released them to our God. After they get bottled up the desired reaction to the concerns can come out as an explosion when it could have been a sweet talk with the Lord and Him giving revelation, insight, security, and peace about the whole ordeal.

God wants us to come to Him and tell Him everything, leaving nothing out. All our concerns should be requests made to Him. Then and only then can we know the truth about everything.

Spending time in prayer with God and studying His Word helps us to know Him and develop a relationship with Him. We were made in His image. The more time we spend together the more we take on His image.

Kimberly Wilkerson

Some things to think about:
- God gives us to His peace
- God wants us to come to Him with our concerns
- Spending time with God helps to develop a closer relationship with Him

How you can apply this to your life: Practice giving your concerns to your Father. Allow Him to take your burdens. Spend time in prayer, talking with your loving Father who wants to give you His peace. Read His Word daily and allow Him to show you His heart.

Digging deeper: Isaiah 41:10 *fear not, for I am with you; be not dismayed, for I am your God; I will strengthen you, I will help you, I will uphold you with my righteous right hand.*

How you can pray about this: Lord Jesus, I love You and I am so grateful for Your promise of peace. I know that I often allow anxiety to take over my thoughts, but I know that You promise to take these burdens from me. Help me to know Your peace, Father.

Remember this: Your loving Father wants you to have His peace.

He is Enough

But he said to me, "My grace is sufficient for you, for my power is made perfect in weakness." Therefore I will boast all the more gladly of my weaknesses, so that the power of Christ may rest upon me.
2 Corinthians 12:9

The world teaches us that we must be strong. In the world, the weak are often trampled on and looked down upon. What we have to remember, as children of God, is that we do not belong to the world, we are a part of the family of God.

If you are a Christian, God sees this differently. He sees your weakest moments as times when He can show you and the world who He is and what He is all about.

I have experienced some significant losses in recent years and in those times I have known what it feels like to be weak to the point of not knowing if I would be able to survive. Yet, God's grace is sufficient.

Seven years ago, I lost my husband of thirty-two years. He was fifty-two. It was the most devastating moment in my life. Later that same year, I lost my sister-in-law. In 2022 I lost my mother-in-law. This year, 2023, I lost my Dad in February and my Mom in May.

I never thought that my story was going to be about loss, but really it isn't about loss. My story, and yours, is about God!

God uses the events of our lives to make us stronger and to draw us closer to Him. We can easily get caught up in our misery during times of suffering, and I have been in that place. But if you can only find a quiet moment to be still and seek after God, He WILL meet you right there in your misery. He provides what we need even in our suffering.

As I write this it has only been weeks since losing my mother. It has been just a few months since losing my father. Because of what God did seven years ago to strengthen and grow my relationship with Him, I have been able to manage these recent losses a little better, because I know Him so much better.

One way that we can impact this broken world and show people our loving Savior is to share our stories of loss and suffering with others.

These days, I am often asked how I am doing and if I need anything. When I think of how to answer these questions, I try to remember how God has walked with me through every trial and I share that with others. His grace is sufficient. His provision is enough. I want others to see this truth for themselves.

When you are suffering, try to remember the suffering of Jesus. Our suffering, though it is often severe, does not compare to the suffering of Christ. He suffered more than we can even comprehend and He did it so that we can be with Him in eternity. This is His perfect provision for whatever we need.

As you read this, know that I am praying for you. I want this time of devotion to encourage you to trust that God can and will meet you wherever you are and walk you through every trial, no matter what it is.

You may think that you deserve your suffering, that you brought this on yourself, and certainly our actions have consequences, but God has a purpose in everything and no pain that we suffer will be wasted.

Allow God to walk with you through your difficult time, seek to grow closer to Him and to trust Him and He will reveal Himself in amazing ways.

God will never force us into a relationship with Him but He wants us to choose Him. He longs to be closer to you because He loves you beyond your own understanding.

His grace is sufficient for whatever you are facing and He will get you through it if you choose Him.

Janis Bolick

Some things to think about:
- God can use our weakness to show His strength to you and to others
- God is always with you in every struggle
- God meets you wherever you are

How you can apply this to your life: It is very easy to get caught up in the struggles of this world. It is important to remember that as believers, we belong to God and He can handle every problem that you will ever know here on earth. Practice trusting Him when you are going through hard times and learn to cast your cares upon Him, for He cares for you.

Digging deeper: 1 Peter 5:6-10 *Humble yourselves, therefore, under the mighty hand of God so that at the proper time he may exalt you, casting all your anxieties on him, because he cares for you. Be sober-minded; be watchful. Your adversary the devil prowls around like a roaring lion, seeking someone to devour. Resist him, firm in your faith, knowing that the same kinds of suffering are being experienced by your brotherhood throughout the world. And after you have suffered a little while, the God of all grace, who has called you to his eternal glory in Christ, will himself restore, confirm, strengthen, and establish you.*

How you can pray about this: Lord Jesus, I am so broken! I want to live my life in a way that glorifies You but I know that often I am going to fall short of that. Help me, Lord! Keep reminding me of how I can walk closer with You. Thank You for saving me and loving me and walking with me through every struggle.

Remember this: God will use your weakness to reveal His strength to you and to others.

God Always Has My Back

My help comes from the LORD, who made heaven and earth. He will not let your foot be moved; he who keeps you will not slumber.
Psalms 121:2-3

This chapter of the Bible has been an inspiration and a source of hope in my life for a very long time. It is also my favorite. I can picture David on his knees, crying out to the heavens, as I have many times before. I can almost hear the stress and anxiety in his voice. *"I will lift up my eyes to the hills-From whence comes my help?"*.

Then comes the reassuring answer to his question. What an awesome and powerful statement!!! When my faith was almost non-existent and I was in the middle of the darkest depths of my addiction, this verse always stirred something in me.

As doubt, guilt, and shame crept in, as it always did, I would continue on to verse 3-4. *"He will not allow your foot to be moved; He who keeps you will not slumber. Behold, He who keeps Israel shall neither slumber nor sleep."* Wow! God always has my back!

Verses 5-8 always put my soul at ease, removing the pressure of me being me. *"The Lord is your keeper; The Lord is your shade at your right hand. The sun shall not strike you by day, nor the moon by night. The Lord shall preserve you from all evil; He shall preserve your soul. The Lord shall preserve your going out and coming in from this time forth, and even forevermore."*

There has never been a time in my life where this verse did not uplift and inspire me. When I was at my lowest, beat down from all the world had to throw at me, God's promise always rings true.

Jason Wallace

Some things to think about:
- God promises to always be near
- His eyes are always on His children
- When your faith is weak, He is strong

How you can apply this to your life: Keep yourself close to God by seeking Him in Scripture and in prayer. Call out to Him in your darkest moments, just as David did, He hears you. Never let your doubt or shame, about your past or even your present situation, be an excuse to put distance between you and God. He longs to be in a close relationship with you.

Digging deeper: Isaiah 30:18 *Therefore the LORD waits to be gracious to you,and therefore he exalts himself to show mercy to you. For the LORD is a God of justice; blessed are all those who wait for him.*

How you can pray about this: Father, it is hard for me to believe that You care so much for me. I know I have failed You so many times, yet You promise to always be near and to always have my back! Thank You so much for how You take care of me in every situation.

Remember this: God is always taking care of you!

The Father's Will

For you save a humble people, but the haughty eyes you bring down. For it is you who light my lamp; the LORD my God lightens my darkness.
Psalms 18:27-28

God is not at our beck and call. We are at His call. Even though God is always with His children and gives them strength, this does not mean that we will always succeed in everyday life.

Sometimes it is God's will for us to lose out on a job or to lose a game.

God is all powerful but He does not give us the right to claim His power whenever we want. We need to submit to the Father's will. God does what He wants, according to His will, not mine or yours. We think we have complete control over our lives if God is with us.

We have to realize God indeed is with us and He alone has complete control over our lives. We must submit to God and yield ourselves to His plan, trusting Him to do what is best for our lives, even if it includes being a failure. He is sovereign over our salvation, our future, our career, every breath.

Our God is the Redeemer of everything in our lives.

Robin Stapleton

Some things to think about:
- We will not always succeed in everything
- We must be submitted to the will of God
- God is in control, we are not

How you can apply this to your life: It is important for us to remember to be submitted to God's will and to trust in His sovereignty. He is the Creator of the universe and He is in complete control of everything that has ever happened, is happening now, or will happen in the future. Learn to trust in Him and seek to be closer to Him so that you will know His will for your life.

Digging deeper: Colossians 3:12 *Put on then, as God's chosen ones, holy and beloved, compassionate hearts, kindness, humility, meekness, and patience,*

How you can pray about this: Lord Jesus, I know that You are in control of everything. I know that I can get caught up in trying to do things myself and not seeking Your will. Help me to remember that I can trust Your sovereignty. Teach me how to be more aware of my own selfish will and show me how to better follow Your will every day.

Remember this: Our God is our Great Redeemer!

True Source of Spiritual Wisdom
For the Lord gives wisdom; from His mouth
come knowledge and understanding.
Proverbs 2:6

Spiritual wisdom only comes from God. Men by nature cannot fully understand spiritual truth. Until man repents and begs God to change his or her life, their eyes will not be open to understand truth or real value. After humbling yourself and repenting to God, to obtain true wisdom, a Christian simply has to ask God for it.

Growing up in the church and going to Sunday School helped me learn a lot about what the Bible says, however, until I asked Christ into my heart, I could read the Bible, but could not really understand it. Once I was saved and the Holy Spirit was in me, I could understand the scripture much better, especially by reading commentaries online.

Think of it like this. God has offered us a treasure chest, but not filled with diamonds and gold coins. This treasure chest is filled with all the valuable information a person will need to walk through their life.

We often find ourselves with no clue as to the right way to handle situations that arise in our daily lives. Instead of looking to God, we look at worldly things for the answer and then get upset if it doesn't work out like we think it should. Rather than getting flustered or irritated, all we need to do is to take a few minutes to go to God in prayer.

You don't need to have some fancy prayer for God. Remember, He knows your heart. Just talk to Him in plain terms and He will hear you.

Jeff Wardsworth

Some things to think about:
- God will give you wisdom and understanding if you recognize who He is and humbly ask Him for it
- He wants to supply you with a treasure of valuable information for your life
- Seeking God and asking for wisdom will help to strengthen your relationship with Him.

How you can apply this to your life: Remember the humility of Jesus when we are seeking something from the Father. Jesus was fully God but while He was here on earth, He constantly sought after God's will in humility and in prayer. We only need a humble heart and a gentle spirit when we come before God and ask Him to provide wisdom and understanding. He provides the rest.

Digging deeper: Psalm 111:10 *The fear of the LORD is the beginning of wisdom; all those who practice it have a good understanding. His praise endures forever!*

How you can pray about this: Lord, we want to know You better and walk in the wisdom that comes from being in a close relationship with You. Teach us how to come to You in humility and show us how to share Your wisdom with others in a way that glorifies You and not ourselves.

Remember this: You don't need fancy words to talk to God, He will hear you.

Chosen

But you are a chosen race, a royal priesthood, a holy nation,
a people for his own possession,
that you may proclaim the excellencies of him who called
you out of darkness into his marvelous light.
1 Peter 2:9

For over 20 years of my life I struggled to belong in this world. All I ever wanted was to belong, to fit in somewhere, to be loved and to have a value or purpose. As a child I was molested, hit on, and always left either with my grandparents or alone at the house because my parents always worked or fought in the evenings when they were at home.

I was an only child, so I had no one to talk to or confide in. Some said I was spoiled, but they did not know what was really going on inside those walls. So, I searched in a lot of wrong places to feel that love and all it did was break me even more.

It took me 45 years of searching, wandering around in the wilderness, if you will, to finally find the love I'd been searching for. To know that the Creator of the universe, the One who made me, hadn't left me all those years. He CHOSE me, He called my name and I heard it.

Not only did He choose me, He said I'm royalty, I'm His beloved, a daughter of the king. That's amazing! I finally belong somewhere and with someone who truly cares for me, enough to save me from myself. I lived a life of self-destruction in my addiction, hopeless and helpless for years. But GOD!!!! I'm A Princess to the Highest King Thank you, Jesus, for saving me when I couldn't save myself!!!!

1 Peter 2:9 says: You (JULIE) are a chosen person, a royal priesthood, a holy nation, a person who belongs to me (God), that you(JULIE) may declare the praises of Him who CALLED you out of darkness into His wonderful light!

Julie McAllister

Some things to think about:
- God never leaves us, He is always with us
- He calls us by name, He chooses us
- As a believer, you belong to the family of God

How you can apply this to your life: Remember that as we struggle through hardships in our lives, God is always with us. Seek to be closer to Him especially during difficult times. Spend time with Him as you read His Word and pray to Him every day. Thank Him for choosing you. If you have not answered His call on your life, seek to hear and accept all that He wants to give you through the gift of salvation.

Digging deeper: Deuteronomy 7:6 *For you are a people holy to the LORD your God. The LORD your God has chosen you to be a people for his treasured possession, out of all the peoples who are on the face of the earth.*

How you can pray about this: Father, I thank You for the beautiful gift of salvation. Thank You for choosing me and saving me. Help me to share the good news of Your son, Jesus, with others so that all might be saved.

Remember this: God has called you by name, you are His!

Weeping And Yet Rejoicing
Weeping may remain for a night,
but rejoicing comes in the morning.
Psalm 30:5

We have been told that there will be trials and tribulations in our lives. No one can escape it or run from it. We have also been told and given promises by Jesus *"...but take heart, for I have already overcome the world"* (John 16:33).

Everyone I know has had a rough patch in their lives. A time where they couldn't fathom what was going to happen next or how to fix their chaos. I went through a very tough storm several years ago. My husband had decided that he wanted a divorce.

The children and I were devastated. We couldn't understand what had happened or why. I explained to our children it was not their fault and they had done nothing wrong. This was an adult problem, and we would get through this together. They were not alone; they still had a dad and we would be okay.

Sometimes no matter how hard one person tries it just isn't meant to be. We just wanted different things. Then I began crying and I would cry until I couldn't cry anymore. I had been through all of the emotions that come with grieving 13 years of marriage.

I started to deal with all of the reasons I was crying, and God began to open my eyes to my faults, the heart of the matter, and to really focus on our children.

Sometimes "a night" can mean literally one night or a lengthy season of time. Only God knows how long it will last but He gives us hope and peace during our storm. God wants us to talk with Him about it, cry about it, be honest with our emotions so He can speak real truth into our hearts and minds. He is trying to grow us in the middle of our chaos.

My "night" ended up lasting two and a half years. I know that sounds horrible, however what God was changing and preparing me for was far greater than the stormy past.

There are moments in our life where doubt creeps in and we begin to sit a little too long in the dark moments. We begin to find comfort in the depressive thoughts or begin to shut down to avoid the storm all together.

When I realized what was happening, I decided to make a change. How could I expect anything to change if I didn't meet God halfway and try to do something different? I couldn't do this on my own, but I couldn't risk just staying the same.

I stopped focusing on the emotions and focused on my habits. I was praying differently and seeking God. I prayed about the type of changes I needed for so long. I focused on the meat of the situation and gave it over to God to figure out.

The weight lifted, the clouds parted, and a new life began. Even in the middle of my storm His light was shining, and I had a peace of mind only He can provide.

When the final court date arrived, I was scared, nervous, anxious, relieved, excited, and back to scared. God whispered I have a new plan and path for your family. Shortly after I was divorced, life changed, and I moved forward.

During this time God introduced me to someone who would change my world. Kenny was someone who had the same family beliefs I did, he cares deeply, is honest, and true to his word. He loved my children as if they were his own and he loved them for who they were. Kenny and I were married later that year.

Do you ever wonder what happens with our prayers? I had forgotten about all of the prayers I said concerning my marriage. God began reminding me of those prayers. Prayers for communication, understanding, love, kindness, etc. Prayers for a spouse who wanted to pray together, go to church with us, etc.

Kenny had been doing all of those things. All that I had asked for and prayed about, laid at my Father's feet had been answered. We are not perfect people by any means, but we had the same foundation and beliefs about relationships.

Our individual relationship with God was the example for our relationship as husband & wife. God had to change me to put me on the path that led to the one he had planned for our family. I went from barely living to rejoicing every blessing in my life, even the dark storms. Rejoice!

Karen MacKinnon

Some things to think about:
- In the middle of our storms, God gives hope
- When we seek God is our storms, He will take care of all of our needs
- When you seek God, He will change you and teach you to rejoice, even in the storms

How you can apply this to your life: Learn to seek God during your storms. These are the times when God will strengthen your faith in so many ways. Remember that you can rejoice during hard times because you know that God is working in every trial. Practice seeking to know what God is doing when you are suffering and rejoice in His will for you.

Digging deeper: James 1:2-4 *Count it all joy, my brothers, when you meet trials of various kinds, for you know that the testing of your faith produces steadfastness. And let steadfastness have its full effect, that you may be perfect and complete, lacking in nothing.*

How you can pray about this: God, it is so hard to go through storms. Help me to find a way to rejoice when I am struggling. Teach me the truth of Your love for me and how You seek to change me and strengthen me through every difficult situation. I know that You are in control and that You do everything for my good, help me to rest in Your promises of hope and peace.

Remember this: God changes you through hard times.

His Only Son

*God so loved the world that he gave his one and only Son,
that whoever believes in him
shall not perish but have eternal life.*
John 3:16

God gave His only Son

What love He has for His sons and daughters. The kind of love we should all have in our hearts and carry with us each day. He didn't have to do that for us, but he cared enough and loved us enough to save us from our sins.

To live a life without sins is impossible, but through our faith and love for His son, we can. We have a Father who can and will. In His word we can find His truth, daily!

While I have been at Freedom Life, I have seen so many miracles. Each day that I arrive here, I am amazed at His presence. As a Christian, we are always challenged daily in our walk with God.

The choices we make, the people we encounter have meaning and purpose to our lives. Freedom Life is at the center of my walk, I am a different person because of my work here. I never knew what love a family can show you in every way.

Kim Brown

Some things to think about:
- God gave the life of His Son so that you could be saved
- Jesus makes it possible for us to be free of our sin
- We are challenged every day in our walk with God

How you can apply this to your life: Remember the sacrifice that God made for you. He allowed Jesus to suffer and die so that you could be with Him in eternity. Jesus chose to go to the cross for you! Reflect on the incredible sacrifice that was made so that all people could be part of the family of God. Accept Jesus into your heart today!

Digging deeper: Isaiah 53:5-6 *But he was pierced for our transgressions; he was crushed for our iniquities; upon him was the chastisement that brought us peace, and with his wounds we are healed. All we like sheep have gone astray; we have turned—every one—to his own way; and the LORD has laid on him the iniquity of us all.*

How you can pray about this: Jesus, I cannot even begin to understand all that You have suffered for me! Thank You for Your sacrifice for me. Forgive me when I so often fail You and help me to repent of the sin in my life. I know that I could never even know You if You had not made a Way for me through the cross. Show me how to share Your gift or salvation with others.

Remember this: God loved you so much that He sent His beloved Son to die for you.

Hard to Believe?

And if the Spirit of him who raised Jesus from the dead
is living in you, he who raised Christ from the dead
will also give life to your mortal bodies
because of his Spirit who lives in you.
Romans 8:11

Have you ever experienced something that was hard to believe? What was it? It could be something you've seen or heard about but still don't understand.

As I grew up there were many things I didn't understand even though I may have seen it. Most likely I still had to ask someone and I often didn't understand even after they explained it to me. Even in my latter years I find some things hard to believe in.

In a famous pastime movie, it was quoted "seeing isn't believing but believing is seeing". The word "believe" is used some 160 times in the bible and means *"to put one's faith in trust, with an implication that actions based on that trust may follow"*.

Jesus in John chapter 11 raises Lazarus from the dead. Lazarus was the brother of Mary and Martha. While on His way to the funeral Martha meets Him and Jesus tells her in John 11:21-25 *Jesus said to her, "Your brother will rise again." Martha answered, "I know he will rise again in the resurrection at the last day." Jesus said to her, "I am the resurrection and the life. The one who believes in me will live, even though they die; and whoever lives by believing in me will never die. Do you believe this?"*

Jesus is asking her if she believes, without seeing. What is your response to His question? Will you believe even when you can't see it or it may seem impossible? Will you trust Jesus? You don't have to see or understand to believe, all you need is to trust in the truth of Jesus to believe. How will you believe in what He is telling you right now?

Paul Cole

Some things to think about:
- Sometimes things are hard to believe
- Believing hard things requires trust
- Will you believe in Jesus without seeing Him?

How you can apply this to your life: The most important decision you will ever make is to believe in Jesus Christ. It will require you to believe in something that you cannot physically see. You will have to put your trust in God and believe that He loves you and wants you with Him for all eternity. Can you take this step in faith?

Digging deeper: Romans 10:9 *because, if you confess with your mouth that Jesus is Lord and believe in your heart that God raised him from the dead, you will be saved.*

How you can pray about this: Lord Jesus, I believe that You are the Messiah Who has come to save the world! I want You to be the Lord of my life and I accept Your gift of salvation. Please forgive me of my sins and make me clean again. Free me from the bondage of sin and show me how to live a life that glorifies You.

Remember this: God wants you in His family!

He Has Made a Way for Us

In my Father's house are many rooms. If it were not so,
would I have told you that I go to prepare a place for you?
And if I go and prepare a place for you, I will come again and
will take you to myself, that where I am you may be also.
John 14:2-3

At some point we all have to decide if we believe. Like really believe. Do you believe that the Word of God is true? Do you know in your heart that He is not even capable of making a mistake?

Does your heart sing with joy knowing that there is no need to worry about the future because He has made a Way for you to be with Him for all eternity?

The words in this passage are from Jesus and He is speaking to His disciples. He is telling them, and us, that He is preparing the Way for us. The disciples did not really understand all that Jesus was sharing with them, yet.

Jesus shares so much with us in chapter 14 of John and in the chapters that follow. He is preparing His disciples for His crucifixion and also for the coming of the Holy Spirit. Yet, they were still confused.

They walked with Him in ministry. They watched Him perform miracles and even performed miracles themselves, yet they struggled to truly believe what He was telling them. When Jesus died and was put in the tomb, they were utterly defeated, for a short time.

After His resurrection came clarity. Now they could understand what He had been telling them. Now they could see how He was making a Way for them to believe.

As you read this passage, I would encourage you to dust off your Bible and read all of the book of John. It is not too hard and not too long, only twenty-one chapters.

God uses His Word to speak to us and to share His heart with us. John 1:1 says: *In the beginning was the Word, and the Word was with God, and the Word was God.* Your Bible is the living Jesus right in your hands! But, do you believe?

Do you want to believe? Are you curious about this place that Jesus says He is preparing for you? Do you have a longing in your heart to know more about the life of Jesus?

I can give you a very easy way to know all that you want to know about God the Father, Jesus, and the Holy Spirit, open your Bible. It is that simple. God will do the rest.

If you approach God through Scripture and you have a soft heart that is willing to listen, God can and will reveal Himself to you and you will be forever changed! If Jesus says that He is preparing a place for you and that He will come again and take you to Himself, please don't resist His call!

Believing is a matter of life and death and it is for all eternity. Nothing else in this whole world is more important than that.

Let Jesus come into your heart. Allow His Spirit to change you, to make you a new creation. You will never regret it!

Janis Bolick

Some things to think about:
- The Bible is the LIVING Word of God
- Do you ever wonder if God is real and if He really cares about you at all?
- It is ok to question God, He wants you to come to Him with your doubts and He can answer every one of them

How you can apply this to your life: How we approach God is not as important as actually choosing to do it. God wants you to seek Him. He longs to have a relationship with you. Almighty God, the Creator of the universe wants you to know Him better! Don't let the devil and this messed up world distract you from knowing who God is and how much He loves you.

Digging deeper: John 14:6-7 *Jesus said to him, "I am the way, and the truth, and the life. No one comes to the Father except through me. If you had known me, you would have known my Father also. From now on you do know him and have seen him."*

How you can pray about this: Lord Jesus, I want to know You! I want Your Spirit to live inside me and provide me with Your guidance and wisdom. I know I cannot earn salvation and I cannot find my way to heaven without You. Thank You, Father, for sending Your Son to make a Way for all of us to be with You. Thank You, Jesus, for sending Your Spirit to be our guide and change our lives!

Remember this: Jesus is the Way!

Keep Coming Back

For the LORD takes pleasure in his people;
he adorns the humble with salvation.
Psalm 149:4

Looking back in my life the past year, I struggled once again with alcohol and drugs. Instead of burying myself in my Bible or in God, I tried to drown myself in things that were bad for me.

I went from healthy people to damning people. And I knew where I was going. I can't say that I didn't care because I was still trying to do the right things.

And I honestly knew that God had me by the hand holding on tight.

And by His grace and mercy, I didn't completely let go of His hand. And I screamed out HIs name and I could feel myself swimming up to the surface of salvation.

But I keep turning my will over to God and my people, my family at Freedom Life.

There I lay my burdens down and check my shame at the door. Because I am always welcomed and loved there!

Kim Miller

Some things to think about:
- It is so easy to fall back into a life of sin
- Satan is looking for ways to distract you from what God is doing in your life
- God's mercy has no end, no matter how many times we mess things up

How you can apply this to your life: Try to always be aware that God is with you and wants to guide you. Seek to find Him in your daily activities and look for how He is working to lead you closer to Him. Remember you have to choose Him, He will not force you to follow Him. You have free will but God desires a relationship with you. The devil is always trying to keep you from seeking after God.

Digging deeper: 1 Peter 5:8-10 *Be sober-minded; be watchful. Your adversary the devil prowls around like a roaring lion, seeking someone to devour. Resist him, firm in your faith, knowing that the same kinds of suffering are being experienced by your brotherhood throughout the world. And after you have suffered a little while, the God of all grace, who has called you to his eternal glory in Christ, will himself restore, confirm, strengthen, and establish you.*

How you can pray about this: Lord Jesus, protect me! Help me to see that You are near. There are so many temptations in this world and it is so easy to do the thing that feels comfortable. I want to choose the path that feels good and distracts me from my pain but I know that You have a better way. Strengthen me in this battle and forgive me of all of the sins of my past.

Remember this: God's promise of forgiveness is our hope

Trust in the Promises of God

I give them eternal life, and they shall never perish; no one will snatch them out of my hand.
John 10:28

This verse is a powerful reminder of the security that we have in Christ. Jesus says that He gives us eternal life, and that no one can take it away from us. This is a promise that we can cling to, no matter what challenges we face in life.

There are many reasons why we can trust this promise. First, Jesus is the Son of God. He is the one who created us and who loves us more than anyone else. He would never abandon us or let us perish.

Second, Jesus died on the cross to pay the penalty for our sins. He took our punishment upon Himself so that we could be forgiven and have eternal life.

Third, Jesus rose from the dead. This proves that He has power over death and that He can keep His promises.

We can trust the promise of eternal life because it is based on the character and promises of Jesus Christ. He is a faithful God who will never break His promises.

This promise of eternal life is a source of great comfort and hope for us. It reminds us that we are loved and secure, no matter what happens in life. We can face the future with confidence, knowing that we have eternal life in Christ.

Jim Smith, Development Director at Freedom Life and serves locally as a minister of music and administration

Some things to think about:
- We can trust this promise, no matter what challenges we face in life
- Since we have eternal life in Christ, we should live for Him.
- We can face the future with confidence, knowing that we have eternal life in Christ.

How you can apply this to your life: Jesus said that He gives us eternal life, and that no one can take it away from us. We can trust in God's promises. We can live for God. We should obey His commands and share the good news of the gospel with others. We can be encouraged. This verse is a source of great comfort and hope for us. It reminds us that we are loved and secure, no matter what happens in life.

Digging deeper: Jeremiah 17:7-8 *Blessed is the man who trusts in the LORD, whose trust is the LORD. He is like a tree planted by water, that sends out its roots by the stream, and does not fear when heat comes, for its leaves remain green, and is not anxious in the year of drought, for it does not cease to bear fruit.*

How you can pray about this: Dear God, Thank You for the promise of eternal life. I know that I can trust You, even when things are tough. Help me to live for You and to share the good news of the gospel with others.

Remember this: God's promises are never broken

Testimonies

Ashley McPeterrs

Those who are actively abusing substances are on a path that has two predictable outcomes, incarceration, or death. Addicts are aware of this truth, yet they find themselves unwilling or unable to break the cycle that keeps them imprisoned. This is true even if they themselves have suffered a near death experience.

Recovery seems impossible to them as they may have tried multiple times on their own to escape their addiction and only found failure. Which in turn often lead to their rejection of other treatment options because they believed that these too would end in failure.

Such is my story. I chose every wrong path and ran from all the right ones. I lost everything repeatedly and still refused help. I pushed away my entire family. Throughout an entire decade I was stuck in the endless cycle of addiction. I started using illicit drugs and alcohol early in my youth. I would often find myself trying to recover without any help. In the beginning of my addiction, there were no obvious consequences for my actions.

So I was blind to the problem. I left my addiction untreated and hidden. One thing I now know is that problems do not remain hidden. Eventually, those underlying problems come to the surface and trigger a reaction. Once I started getting in trouble it seemed like the charges and convictions would never stop. I would get locked up in county jail and sober up for a little bit. But when I was released I found myself in all those familiar places.

Normally, it did not take long for all those old habits to creep back in. My recidivism rate climbed. I ended up with thirty or so misdemeanor convictions and two felony convictions. I had to go to prison for nineteen months. That experience should have changed me but it did not. It is like I was chasing death instead of life.

I was addicted to self-destruction. Living in chaos was the only pattern that seemed like comfort. I struggled so long in trap houses that it became a sense of normalcy to me. My tolerance for drugs was so high that I almost had to die to enjoy my high. I had to literally meet my own death to wake up.

Then one day it happened, I overdosed and almost lost my life. Thankfully, my neighbor was home and came and performed CPR until the EMS arrived. I woke up with emergency responders and sheriff department officers all around me. I had never felt more embarrassed by my addiction than I did at that moment. I was caught red handed and could no longer hide my affliction.

I remember my death like it was yesterday. It is still vivid to me. I can feel the warm embrace I felt while slipping from this world to the next. A voice, only heard by me, said, soon all your pain would be over. The next thing I was aware of was a sense of falling back into my body.

This was an eye-opening experience. I came close to losing everyone I loved. It helped me finally to get a grip on the reality of my situation. I was either going to let my addiction control me or I was going to seek recovery. My life changed immensely after that day. I chose recovery and recovery became my newfound passion.

The first step in my recovery was choosing a reentry program. Thankfully, a friend referred me to Freedom Life Ministries. Freedom life is a Christ centered reentry program, something that initially scared me a bit. But it was here I came to realize there was a greater power than myself that I could trust. I started going to regular meetings and attending classes at Freedom Life Ministries. I have finally found a support system of trained counselors and other recovering addicts all around me encouraging me toward success.

I began the process of identifying my underlying mental health issues with guided counseling. I learned I had to discover the root of all my problems; all my brokenness within, to break the cycle that was constantly leading me to relapse. I cannot say this was the easy part. I had to define my triggers and create a list of coping mechanisms for each trigger. Slowly, I am starting to find some positives in all the negatives that have encased my life. I have also come to the realization that I have hurt many people and I am beginning the painful process of seeking their forgiveness.

I know now that recovery happens easier when you have someone in your life you chose to be accountable too. I have a sponsor who meets with me regularly holding me accountable for my actions. I also join with other recovering addicts in Celebrate Recovery rally's which help me keep my faith alive. I feel renewed by the positive team I now have guiding and encouraging me. I no longer suffer in silence. It has now been almost two years since my last taste. I am close to being reunited with my children. I am still retraining my brain but now my future is filled with hope.

Jeff Wardsworth

Choosing Christ Over Crime
"Submit yourselves therefore to God. Resist the devil, and he will flee from you."
James 4:7

Growing up in a strong, conservative Southern Baptist home, going to church and knowing the Bible was not an option, it was a requirement. Being raised in such a strict environment, I soon found myself resenting authority and longing for the freedom that my friends seemed to have.

As the years went by, I found using drugs and alcohol just made life more tolerable. My true addiction, though, was not conforming to what society said I should and consequently, I chose to break every rule I could. I got such a rush off of breaking laws and not getting caught.

After being convicted of multiple felonies, God convicted me of my sins and I truly repented. Even though Christ saved me, I still had to face society's laws and was sentenced to eighty-six months in prison.

Being incarcerated for so many years taught me another valuable lesson. Either I needed to change my ways and serve Christ or just resign myself to a life of crime, which would lead to multiple prison sentences and a life of total physical and emotional bondage.

After being released from prison for over twenty years now, I feel that Christ has led me to a life of service by helping other men who are currently incarcerated and that are being released back into society.

While Jesus Christ can change your life and make you a new person, He also gives each one of us a choice of free will. Every single day, I have to choose to do the right thing.

Even though Satan is constantly badgering me, I have to choose to walk in truth. I choose to read my Bible daily and I choose to pray many times during the day. It is ultimately up to me to try and develop a closer relationship with Christ.

Jason Wallace

It never ceases to amaze me how God is continually putting the pieces of our lives together, even when we are not aware of what is going on. McDowell county jail is where I found myself on December 16, 2019, convicted and awaiting transport to state prison. This was the result of a twenty-five year addiction with a foundation of a lifetime of brokenness.

I had already decided that I wanted out of that life, but I had no idea how I was going to be able to pull that off. I felt alone. I had exhausted myself and pretty much every opportunity that had ever been afforded to me. I had spent my whole life running from the very thing that was going to save me. GOD'S LOVE.

This day was a little different though because little did I know I was going to experience a little taste of that and it would change my life!!! As I laid on my bunk that morning, I heard all the cell doors pop and we exited them to find Heartcry, Freedom Life's music ministry, awaiting to bless us with a concert and testimonies. Even as someone that was extremely resistant to anything "Jesus", I felt a very comforting tug inside of myself as I realized that this ministry may be the lifeline that I so desperately needed in my life.

On the day of my release from prison, my parole officer dropped me off on the doorstep of Freedom Life. I had nothing but the prison clothes I had on my back and an unopened bible that I received while in prison.

At that time I fully submitted to the year long, moral based program (they have moral or spiritual based programs) and they began meeting my immediate needs. This included housing, clothing, food, and transportation just to name a few. What a relief and a blessing but the best was yet to come.

Then came secondary needs, assigning me a case manager to guide me through the many challenges that justice involved individuals face. Next, they put me on the Freedom pressure washing team as a volunteer where I was given hands-on training and a quality mentor. Throughout the following months I was introduced to the love of Christ and invited to start attending church.

After attending the first service I was hooked and have attended a service every time the doors open since!!! The Lord continued to bless me with a great job at Marion Fabric and Upholstery, a place that partners with Freedom Life, to help men transform their lives and transition into society.

That was two years ago and today I am blessed to work for the same ministry that helped save my life. I am so thankful for all the people that allowed God's love to shine through them along the way. It has been an awesome experience getting to know the love of Christ while growing into the man that I was born to be. A son of God and a co-heir with Christ!!!

Michael Fox

God has thoroughly changed my perspective of who He is, and who I am in Him. I am fearfully and wonderfully made in His image. I was not made to fit into an image of Christian according to the world's standards. The only image for any of us truly is that of His Son Jesus.

I spent over twenty years in addiction. I used it all to numb the pain of my own brokenness. I struggled with worthlessness and rejection. I found myself listening to the wrong voices and believing the lies of the enemy.

I found myself incarcerated in 2013 and Jesus met me there, where I was. He came into the midst of my mess to give me a message of His love for me. I grew up in church but never truly knew the love of God until I found myself in jail. There is nothing that can separate us from the love of God.

I am now alive as I have never been and free from the bonds of addiction. While incarcerated I met Danny Hampton and Scott Kelley. They showed me through their actions just how much God loved me.

Through Godly counsel from Danny, God has turned my rejection into acceptance and is showing me just how much He values me.

It was there that Danny invited me to join Heart Cry and be a part of Freedom Life Ministries. It is truly a privilege and honor to be able to be a voice of encouragement to those battling the same struggles I have faced.

I love seeing the miracle of God's grace and mercy in the lives of those around me and look forward to seeing what He is going to do tomorrow. God is not done.

He has always been faithful in my life, working things out behind the scenes that I never thought I would see. And I can't wait to see what He is going to do with this ministry.

Steven Davis

It's not how you start, it's how you finish! That's the slogan at our church. The first time that I heard it, I thought to myself "Wow, that's my life summed up in eight words." Paul tells us in 2 Timothy 4:7 That he had fought a good fight, he had finished his course, and that he had kept the faith. It wasn't until after his personal experience with the Son of God on the Damascus Road he became the apostle Paul.

Much like Paul I didn't start out too well in life . Eventually I had my personal experience with the Lord. The Bible says in proverbs that the fear of the Lord is the beginning of wisdom. Both of my parents were addicts. My parents split when I was seven and mom was addicted to pills while dad was drinking, pills and then manufacturing crystal meth. I started using at age twelve and my life was consumed by drugs from that point on.

After countless near death experiences, collecting money, getting in car wrecks, fights, getting stabbed, and bleeding out internally from using I still hadn't woken up. I felt like it was just my heritage to be a dope dealer. All that stuff was like an honor to me that I had made it through it. I have been hooked on everything from weed to meth, If it got you high I was in. The devil had such a strong hold on me. His plan was that I would die and go to hell.

But God was merciful and came after me. Even when I was in the dope houses he came looking for me. In jail He was there. No matter where I was He was there. No matter what I did He was there.

When everyone else left me and I had nothing, He was there! Jesus said *"behold I stand at the door and knock. If any man will open I will come in and sup with him and he with me."* The bible says that it's not His will that any should perish.

I had no idea why my life was so hard. Why things were the way that they were but I've come to realize that God was working it for my good! I would get cases of the do better but that wasn't going to cut it, He wanted all of me! Not a lot to ask considering He spoke the world into existence. We are His creation.

After over twenty years of running, I surrendered to the Lord. January 19, 2017 is the last time that I touched meth. I owe it all to Him. The Bible says you reap what you sow, and when you get saved God cleans that spiritual man up right then, but this carnal man has to work at it every single day.

Paul said we have to die to the flesh daily. The bible also says in 1 John 2:1 *"My little children I would that ye sin not. And if any man sin we have an advocate with the father, Jesus Christ the righteous."*

On September 19,2019 I answered my call to preach the gospel, fully devoted unto the Lord and God has blessed me more than I could ever tell you since then. He pulled me out of a horrible pit, placed my feet on a solid rock (Jesus), and established my goings.

The Lord has blessed me with a wife, a home, a motorcycle, a truck and a family. I don't worry about having money to eat, or where I'm going to sleep. I never ever have to be dope sick again! I see my children regularly. The things I missed out on, like getting to pick my kids up from school, I get to do now. It's not about material things, but Jesus.

John 10:10 says *"the thief cometh not but for to kill, steal and destroy,"* Jesus said *"I am come that they may have life and have it more abundantly."* The devil came and took everything but when I turned my heart to Jesus He abundantly pardoned me and has blessed me with more than I could imagine.

Seek the Lord with your whole heart and He will give you the desires of your heart. Remember in your walk with the Lord that you can do all things through Christ who strengthens you, and it's not how you started this thing it's how you finish!

Robin Stapleton

My name is Robin and I'm a grateful believer in Jesus Christ. My recovery began with anxiety, depression, and codependency, but now I am dealing with a lot of childhood trauma that I have stuffed all of my life. One of the Bible verses that has always stuck with me is Jeremiah 29:11. *"I know the plans I have for you, declares the Lord. plans to prosper you and not to harm you. Plans to give you a hope and a future."*

I was born into what I thought was a caring home. My parents gave me the love they knew how to give. I do remember going to church as a child, but never as a family. I do remember accepting Jesus into my life at the age of fifteen. At that point I was craving to have the love of God in my life.

Then when I was sixteen my whole life was turned upside down. I was molested by a teacher who had asked me to help grade papers during my lunch time. I kept this a secret all my life. By keeping this stuffed for so long and not sharing my pain, I felt sad and worthless. I was shy and very angry with God for letting this happen to me. The bottom line is that it put me into a deep depression. I isolated myself which caused all my anxiety.

I was engaged right out of high school to get married to the man I thought I was in love with, but really I had no love for him at all. It was just a way to get out of my house sooner. One thing I do regret is not communicating my past with my husband before getting married. It could have possibly saved my marriage. I do have two wonderful children and seven grandchildren who have been a blessing to me in my life.

After my divorce in 1988 I pretty much turned my back on the Lord. I still believed He was there but at that time my walk didn't match my talk. I was still wanting to do things my own way no matter the price. At that time in my life my kids were with their grandparents a lot as I would work and go out to the bars with my friends. This lasted about two to three months then I decided this was not the kind of life for me or my kids. I still was not fully walking with the Lord but I was out in the bars all night. I was working full time in Columbus, Ohio and being the mom I needed to be.

Then I was asked if I wanted to attend an Emmaus walk weekend which is a seventy-two hour Christian walk with the Lord and at that time I was more than ready to turn my life back over to God. During my walk I had recommitted my life over to Christ and began walking with the Lord day and night.

Later that same year, I was in a severe wreck where it could have ended my life, but I know by the grace of God, He was showing me that He was still there and in control of my life. I walked away with a scratch on my right hand and a black eye. The enemy was trying to stop me from my joy but that didn't happen. Going through this experience showed me what our God can do.

Well this lay heavy on my heart even to this day that I have been codependent on my son, Adam, a lot. When he got in trouble with the law and ended up in jail, I bailed him out instead of letting him stand on his own two feet. Then he lost his job so he moved back home to stay. I feel I enabled him by letting him move home because it gave him no responsibilities.

In July of 2016 I went to Marysville, Ohio to spend time with my other grandchildren for a week. I ended up in the hospital with what they thought was a heart attack, but it was a severe case of anxiety and depression. My life changed a lot. I had to move back home with my parents because my anxiety and depression were so bad that I could not be alone.

Until I moved back home I had not realized how much me and my mother did not get along. It was a daily battle and I felt completely unloved by my own parents. I would stay in my room most of the time. My depression got worse and I began to think about suicide and I cried all the time. But then I thought that this is not God's plan for me, He has a hope and a future in place and I have seven grandchildren to see graduate!

I would go to work but would barely get anything done. I was late all the time and really did not care about my life. It got even worse so in January of the next year I quit so that I could begin to work on myself.

In November I was asked if I would be interested in attending the Celebrate Recovery program at my church back home. I agreed to attend one time because I did not think I needed a program. Boy was I wrong, almost two years later I was still finding things to work on. I had been sick for over two years and after many appointments, doctors finally figured out that I had a bad gallbladder and needed surgery.

I was so scared because it had been thirty-one years since I had been in surgery. I was not sure if God was even there. But He was with me every step of the way! I am now able to eat again and I am so amazed by what God has done in my life. He is still helping me to this day.

In December I began my first step study class with seven other women and could not believe how deep God had taken me on my journey with Him. It was amazing to see God work in my life after so many years of putting God on the back burner. I feel that by working through my steps, I now want to read my Bible, pray, and journal daily. The CR program has helped me so much and I am happier now. I love to help people who are struggling but more than that, it has helped me to be more comfortable talking in front of people and sharing my story.

In September of 2018 I decided to move to North Carolina to be with my twin grandchildren who I have not seen for two years. I had been praying about it for a while. I know that it was the right move, even though my van broke down when I got here. I had to go on faith and buy a car.

I had to say goodbye to all of my siblings which was so much harder than I thought it would be. I have become so much closer to my sister now than ever before. God has been working with me through my church and helping with the Celebrate Recovery program. I have been leading the step study which has been wonderful.

In July of 2019 I moved into a homeless shelter because where I was staying was not a good environment for me. Then in September I applied to go to Grace Home in Santee, South Carolina.

Then in January of 2020 I went to Vessels of Mercy for a year which is a discipleship program. While in this program, I learned who I am in Christ. After I came home from Vessels and continued in more intensive therapy, I realized how much childhood trauma I still had to deal with.

My move has brought me closer to my mom and we now have a bond that we never had before. I get phone calls from her now which never happened when I lived five minutes away from her. Now she calls just to say hello or even "I love you" which has never happened before. I know God is working in this relationship and in my life. I just needed to be patient and let Him take the wheel. Being patient is hard for me.

I will end with this verse, Romans 12:2: *Don't copy the behavior and customs of this world, but let God transform you into a new person by changing the way you think. Then you will learn to know God's will for you, which is good and pleasing and perfect.* My walk with God has changed so much ever since my move. I have gotten closer to God and want to know more about His love for me.

I encourage everyone who is ready to sign up for a step study which will help you to go deeper with your walk with the Lord and to reach out to a sponsor or accountability person that you can reach out to throughout your week.

Julie McAllister

My name is Julie McAllister and I am a person in long term recovery. I struggled with my addiction for well over twenty years. I was looking for love in all the wrong places, as the song goes. I was a very broken little girl who just wanted to please the ones I loved so that in return they would love me back.

It took me two failed marriages and many men in between to come to the end of myself at the age of forty-five and to realize I first had to love myself. I had to be broken of everything I ever knew and built back up in a whole new life, a new way of thinking and living.

The year 2016 was horrible to me, my marriage of twenty-five years was ending, my home of forty-three years burned to the ground and my whole identity went up in flames along with it. My parents, whom I had been taking care of, went into a nursing home and I was forbidden to see them. The choices I had made over the past few years led to that.

I blamed myself for breaking a promise I had made to my mother. I promised she would never live in a nursing home. Of course who was I kidding? I had broken thousands of promises over the years to not just her, but my two sons and my husband.

You see I was brought up knowing God (in my head) and all His stories, but I was running from that, because as a child I was molested, in my home I was physically abused, talked down to, belittled. I felt very unloved and unwanted.

I had seen my father hit my mother and myself. I knew he cheated, so for me, I thought that's what love was. My very first boyfriend was the same way, abusive and a cheater, again I thought this was love. I stayed for two years and then left and within six months I had moved on to someone else, gotten pregnant and married, to a stranger basically.

Needless to say he was the very same way. I knew I didn't want this for my son, I didn't want him to become like "them". At one point my husband went to prison for stabbing my father and beating me. He had beat me so badly that while he was there I divorced him. But also while he was in there I had met someone else, someone not like all the others.

This guy protected me, showed me kindness and for once I felt "loved". Two weeks after my divorce was final I married this man. Four years into our marriage and after having another son, I had to have a hysterectomy. Two weeks later I came home to my husband lying on the floor having a seizure, which turned out to be a massive brain tumor. He had to have surgery or he would die.

But no one told me that the man I married would literally die on the table and I would be given a new man, this tumor had turned him into someone I didn't know. Or maybe it just unmasked the person that was buried deep down. Either way our lives changed, forever!! This led to our addiction to opioids.

For years we functioned, held jobs, had cars, even owned our home and the land it was on. But eventually it caught up to us, one was never enough, and neither was twenty. Two people and a bad habit! Lots of fighting at this point, I worked all the time to avoid coming home and he started looking for others to give to him what I wasn't.

Truthfully, our marriage died long before I walked away, probably ten to fifteen years before. Lots of resentment and hate built up between the both of us. By 2016 when we literally lost it all, he left me on the streets for three nights. I slept on the church steps that feed homeless people. They didn't see me as a junkie, they saw me as just Julie.

I began going there and three months later I was baptized, but in my mind, I had done something good and it was cause for celebration. So, I went back to the tent and got high. My situation hadn't changed and the stressors of everyday life on the streets had gotten to me so bad I didn't know who I was nor care to know. I hated life, I hated people and I started going to jail on what seemed like a monthly basis.

I got to the point of becoming hopeless, tired and I didn't see a way out. Nowhere! Until I ran into an old neighbor one day who saw me walking in town. She told me of this place in Marion called the Friendship Home and said they would help me. Well I asked the pastor of the church if someone could take me there because I was done with life and I knew something had to change.

So that Monday I left, told no one, not my kids who were grown at this point and yes I was the mom who walked my kids into the same life I was living. I felt so much shame and guilt and I knew why they felt the way they did towards me.

I had let them down, I had let myself down. But I was determined to fix this!! No matter what I had to do, I didn't want them to have the life I had had, things had to change and I was going to fight for that.

Two weeks after coming to McDowell County and the Friendship Home, I met Danny and Melissa at Freedom Life, and when I saw that God had come down and planted himself in Danny Hampton, it had me in awe! Who were these people and how did they know so much about me?

Well needless to say May, 2017 I started going to counseling there and it was counseling like I had never had before. This time it was hitting me to the core of my being, changing my whole perception on life and who I was. It's Christian based and between them and the substance abuse classes I was taking I was starting to understand what was happening and why I did some of the things I did.

Then one day while at Friendship House, I saw my husband on FaceBook with another woman and that broke me all over again. I relapsed! But the case manager at the Friendship Home had me call Melissa and tell her what happened and they both asked me to consider going to a Christian rehab in Santee SC, so I did. I felt lost, lonely and very angry all over again. Why not go, what did I have to lose, absolutely nothing, I had already lost it all!!

So I left in November of 2017 and five weeks in it hit me like a ton of bricks. I surrendered it all, every bit of it, the good, the bad and definitely the ugly. I started liking myself again and I started building a relationship with God. Not just in my head but in my heart. I came back in March of 2018. It had been five months since I had seen my sons. One was in jail and the other was still on the streets. I asked them both to read the book of John. God's love for us.

Of course this was foreign to them because I never talked to them about God as children. So Melissa told me to love from a distance and let them see my walk, so that's exactly what I did. As hard as it was to want to go and help them I had to let them see my change. And in May the son that was in jail asked if Freedom Life would help him and they said yes. He came and stayed at their transition house and then went to the men's version of Grace Home, where I had been, and wow!! He's almost five years clean of heroin and meth.

I am six years clean of any substances. Four months later my oldest son came. He said he wanted that same twinkle in his eye that we had. He too came to the transition house and to Hebron and now he's four years clean of meth and heroin.

The three of us now have a wonderful life, a healthy relationship, and our family is restored. Just like Danny and Melissa said at the very first meeting I had with them. God had restored what Satan had taken from us!! Yes, I had to divorce my husband of twenty-five years. He wasn't ready for that change and still isn't six years later. But it's God's timing and I had to give it to Him and know that He has us and this is exactly His plan for me.

This verse is my life verse that I'm sharing because it helps me to remember that I am loved and my old life is gone and that's ok because today is a new day and I'm a new person, I can let the worries of yesterday go. I hope it helps you let go as well.

2 Corinthians 5:17 says:

Therefore, if anyone (me) *is in Christ, he* (she, me, Julie) *is a new creation; the old has gone and the NEW has come!!!!*

Anita Miller

I grew up in a very dysfunctional family - my mom was a workaholic and my dad was an alcoholic. My second oldest sibling was addicted to drugs which led my brother the same way. My mom and dad fought every time their paths crossed and I was the youngest of four.

I was molested and raped and nothing was ever said. I grew older thinking that it was ok to be touched and taken advantage of. I was twelve when I had my first breakdown. I was in and out of doctor's offices and hospitals for psychiatric purposes. I was put on all kinds of medicines and was admitted into Broughten Hospital for my first suicide attempt.

I was there three months and my mom married the man that had sexually abused me. When I got pregnant at fourteen I was forced to have an abortion which led to the suicide attempt at fifteen. I turned sixteen and signed myself out of Broughten and went and got a job and stayed with a friend and was introduced to a man who was nine years older than me.

We dated for two weeks and he asked me to marry him. I accepted because I felt it was my way out of having to go back home. I got pregnant at seventeen and had my first child at seventeen. I started drinking heavily and did whatever drugs my husband put in front of me. A couple years went by and I had another child. Still doing whatever I could.

My husband started being very abusive and was sleeping around with whoever he could. All of my so-called friends. I was sexually abused and had another child. I truly thought that I was supposed to stay in my marriage because of the vows I made. I sank into very deep depression and was in and out of mental wards for breakdowns brought on by the abuse.

I moved me and my kids around so many times but I always went back to thinking things would get better. They only got worse after I went back. Things got to where my mind was spinning out of control like a tornado. I got pregnant again and my husband drove me and our three children to a abortion clinic in Charlotte and forced me to have an abortion - that pushed me over the edge and I was again admitted into a psych hospital in Charlotte.

At this point I was forced to sell my body and forced to have sex with numerous couples and always got my butt beat after each time. I got so overwhelmed I tried suicide again. While I was recovering a pastor came to see me and after seventeen years of marriage, he explained that God would never want me to be beaten and abused the way I was.

I got into church and my husband did too. I cried for help over and over but never accepted Christ. The drugs entered again and led to the end of the marriage. I fought for three years for a divorce and during this time I met a man that treated me so well. He lived three hours away and had a great job and a beautiful home. I left everything- including my children to get away from it all.

When my divorce came final I got remarried. I was granted visitation with my children and this man was a great stepfather. We were married for five years and I got pregnant and Jacob was born early and his heart stopped during his birth.

My life got out of control yet again. I turned to alcohol and drugs and started my crazy living again. Neglecting him and everything around me. Four more years went by and I got pregnant again and had a precious little boy. At this point I thought my life was complete.

When I was trying so hard to be a better person my health started getting difficult. My back and neck were in bad shape and I got put on pain pills along with all the other meds I was taking. The emptiness within was just there and I fell back into abusing everything and everyone. Abandoning everyone including my children for the drugs. Sleeping around and not caring for anything or anyone.

My marriage ended after fifteen years. He came home and I had another man in our home. He took Matthew and put me out of the house with what I could carry. I lost everything. My mom and daughter came to get me from a neighbor's house and I came back to my mom's. I just kept getting deeper and deeper in my addiction. I became the lowest of lows. Selling dope, lying, cheating, stealing.

My mom got very sick with cancer and when she passed away my world crumbled around me. I lost everything. I didn't even feel anymore. I just stayed numb… Then I got tired, so tired. I was living in my van and I started to realize that there had to be something better.

My daughter had been staying at the Friendship Home and was getting ready to move into her new home. She had been trying to get me to come but I was not going to ruin her recovery. So when she moved out into her new home I moved into the friendship home.

I still used and got kicked out after a few days but they didn't turn their backs on me. They got me in Addact in Black Mountain. It was a fourteen day rehab. I smoked on my way there and they drug tested me and I had to be in detox before rehab.

The day I was to go to rehab, I got a room mate and she had covid. I was put in quarantine for fourteen days. Well I was in that room with a lot of time to think and that's when I accepted Jesus into my heart. I was not there by chance. I was chosen. Jesus had been waiting on me throughout every situation in my life. The fourteen days ended and I went to the rehab side.

I spent a total of thirty-five days there. I graduated and came back to Friendship Home as a new person. I started attending church and reading God's Word. I was still struggling with emptiness in my heart. I was asked to go to a faith based rehab in Santee SC. Grace Home. A ministry for women who are addicted to drugs and alcohol. I went with bells on.

I knew about Jesus and I knew what He had done for me. But while I was at the Grace Home I got to know Him. I got knowledge of what it meant to surrender it all to Him. I started my relationship with Jesus! Praising His name in everything.

My health caused me to have to leave early but I got what I went for. I went back to the Friendship Home and graduated my classes there and got an apartment of my own. Seeking medical attention for several situations, I was diagnosed with cancer. I was taken to hospital thinking I had pulled a muscle. That's when they found a mass on my kidney.

I left the hospital and went to a celebration at church but ended up back in the hospital from the pain. I had cracked two ribs and they sent me to Asheville for further testing. There they found the places on my lungs and bones and gave me a death sentence.

Well they did a biopsy on my lung and when we got results it showed no cancer. My Jesus healed me of lung and bone cancer. I'm still facing surgery on my kidney but my faith and my trust is in the Lord. I have moved into a new home beside my daughter and I'm serving the Lord with every breath I take. My relationship with my Jesus grows stronger and stronger. I'm so grateful for His love.

Made in the USA
Middletown, DE
02 August 2023